THIS BOOK BELONGS TO

The Library of

....

....

Thanks ever so much to each of my cherished readers for investing the time to read this book!

I know you could have picked from many other books, but you chose this one. So, a big thanks for reading all the way to the end. If you enjoyed this book or received value from it, I'd like to ask you for a favor. Please take a few minutes to **post an honest and heartfelt review on** Amazon.com. Your support does make a difference and helps to benefit other people.

Thanks!

Table of Contents

SUMMARY

The Delightful World of Culinary Amigurumi: The Delightful World of Culinary Amigurumi is a fascinating and creative realm where the art of crochet meets the culinary world. Amigurumi, a Japanese term meaning crocheted or knitted stuffed toy, has gained immense popularity in recent years. This unique craft involves creating adorable and miniature stuffed toys using crochet techniques.

In the culinary amigurumi world, crochet enthusiasts take inspiration from various food items and transform them into charming and whimsical creations. From fruits and vegetables to pastries and desserts, the possibilities are endless. Imagine crocheting a tiny watermelon slice, a cute cupcake, or even a miniature sushi roll. These delightful creations not only showcase the creativity and skill of the crocheter but also bring joy and smiles to those who see them.

The process of creating culinary amigurumi involves selecting the perfect yarn colors to mimic the textures and shades of the chosen food item. Crocheters carefully study the details of the food, such as the shape, texture, and even the tiny seeds or sprinkles, to ensure that their amigurumi creation looks as realistic as possible. They use various crochet stitches and techniques to achieve the desired outcome, paying attention to every intricate detail.

One of the most exciting aspects of culinary amigurumi is the opportunity to experiment with different yarn types and textures. For example, using a fluffy yarn can create the illusion of whipped cream or frosting, while a shiny yarn can mimic the glossy appearance of a glazed donut. Crocheters often mix and match yarns to achieve the desired effect, resulting in truly unique and eye-catching creations.

The culinary amigurumi community is a vibrant and supportive one, with enthusiasts sharing their patterns, tips, and tricks with each other. Online platforms and social media groups dedicated to this craft provide a space for crocheters to connect, inspire, and learn from one another. These platforms also offer a wide range of patterns and tutorials, making it accessible for beginners to dive into the world of culinary amigurumi.

The appeal of culinary amigurumi extends beyond just crochet enthusiasts. These adorable creations make perfect gifts for food lovers, children, and anyone who appreciates the art of handmade crafts. They can be used as keychains, bag charms, or simply displayed as decorative items. The versatility and charm of culinary amigurumi make them a delightful addition to any collection or a unique way to add a touch of whimsy to everyday

Bringing Breakfast, Lunch, and Dinner to Your Crochet Needle: Are you tired of having to put down your crochet needle every time you need to prepare a meal? Do you wish you could continue working on your project while enjoying a delicious breakfast, lunch, or dinner? Well, we have the perfect solution for you!

Introducing the innovative concept of bringing breakfast, lunch, and dinner to your crochet needle. With this revolutionary idea, you no longer have to choose between satisfying your hunger and continuing your crochet work. Now, you can have the best of both worlds!

Imagine waking up in the morning, grabbing your crochet needle, and sitting down to enjoy a scrumptious breakfast without having to put your project aside. Whether you prefer a hearty bowl of oatmeal, a stack of fluffy pancakes, or a plate of eggs and bacon, you can now savor your meal while effortlessly working on your crochet masterpiece.

But it doesn't stop there. When lunchtime rolls around, you no longer have to interrupt your creative flow to prepare a meal. Instead, you can have a delicious and nutritious lunch delivered right to your crochet station. From fresh salads and sandwiches to warm soups and wraps, the options are endless. You can indulge in a satisfying meal while your crochet needle keeps moving, ensuring that you make progress on your project without any interruptions.

And when dinnertime arrives, you can say goodbye to the hassle of having to stop crocheting to cook a meal. Instead, you can have a delectable dinner delivered straight to your doorstep. Whether you're craving a comforting bowl of pasta, a flavorful stir-fry, or a mouthwatering steak, you can enjoy a restaurant-quality meal while continuing to work on your crochet project.

Not only does this concept save you time and effort, but it also allows you to fully immerse yourself in your crochet work. By eliminating the need to pause and prepare meals, you can maintain your focus and concentration, resulting in more productive and enjoyable crochet sessions.

So, how does it work? Simply place your order for breakfast, lunch, or dinner from a variety of local restaurants or meal delivery services. Specify your crochet station as the delivery location, and voila! Your meal will be brought directly to you, allowing you to seamlessly combine your love for crochet with your need for nourishment.

In conclusion, bringing breakfast, lunch, and dinner to your crochet needle is a game-changer for all crochet enthusiasts. It allows you to enjoy delicious meals without having to sacrifice your progress on your crochet project.

How to Navigate and Utilize This Flavorful Crochet Guide: Welcome to this flavorful crochet guide! Whether you're a beginner or an experienced crocheter, this guide is designed to help you navigate and utilize all the resources and techniques available to create beautiful and delicious crochet projects.

First and foremost, let's talk about navigation. This guide is divided into different sections, each focusing on a specific aspect of crochet. From basic stitches to advanced techniques, you'll find everything you need to know to enhance your crochet skills. To make it easier for you to find what you're looking for, we've included a table of contents at the beginning of the guide. This will allow you to quickly jump to the section that interests you the most.

Now, let's delve into the utilization of this guide. One of the key features of this guide is the step-by-step instructions provided for each crochet technique. Whether you're learning how to create a basic chain stitch or attempting a more complex stitch pattern, you'll find detailed instructions accompanied by clear and concise illustrations. These visuals will help you understand the techniques better and ensure that you're on the right track.

In addition to the instructions, this guide also includes helpful tips and tricks to enhance your crochet experience. These tips range from choosing the right yarn and hook size for your project to troubleshooting common mistakes. By following these suggestions, you'll be able to achieve better results and avoid unnecessary frustrations.

Furthermore, this guide offers a variety of crochet patterns for you to try. These patterns cater to different skill levels and project types, ensuring that there's something for everyone. Whether you're interested in making a cozy blanket, a stylish hat, or a cute amigurumi toy, you'll find patterns that suit your preferences. Each pattern includes a list of materials needed, detailed instructions, and sometimes even video tutorials to guide you through the process.

To make your crochet journey even more enjoyable, we've included some fun and creative ideas for customizing your projects. From adding embellishments and appliques to experimenting with color combinations, these suggestions will help you put your own personal touch on your crochet creations.

Lastly, this guide encourages you to explore and experiment with different crochet techniques and styles. While the instructions and patterns provided are a great starting point, don't be afraid to let your creativity shine. Crochet is a versatile craft that allows for endless possibilities, so feel free to adapt and modify the techniques and patterns to suit your own unique vision.

Ensuring a Fun and Fulfilling Amigurumi Journey: Amigurumi, the Japanese art of crocheting or knitting small stuffed animals or creatures, has gained immense popularity in recent years. It offers a unique and creative way to express oneself through yarn and create adorable and huggable toys. However, embarking on an amigurumi journey can sometimes be overwhelming, especially for beginners. Therefore, it is essential to ensure that your amigurumi journey is not only fun but also fulfilling.

To begin with, it is crucial to choose the right patterns and projects that align with your skill level and interests. There are countless amigurumi patterns available online, ranging from simple and beginner-friendly designs to more complex and intricate ones. It is advisable to start with simpler patterns if you are a beginner and gradually progress to more challenging projects as you gain confidence and experience. This way, you can avoid frustration and enjoy the process of creating your amigurumi.

Furthermore, investing in high-quality materials is essential for a fulfilling amigurumi journey. Choosing the right yarn and hooks can significantly impact the outcome of your project. Opt for yarn that is soft, durable, and suitable for amigurumi projects. Acrylic yarn is a popular choice due to its affordability and wide range of colors. Additionally, selecting the appropriate hook size is crucial to achieve the desired tension and stitch definition. Experimenting with different yarns and hooks can help you discover your preferences and enhance your amigurumi skills.

In addition to materials, having the right tools and accessories can make your amigurumi journey more enjoyable. Stitch markers, tapestry needles, and stuffing tools are some of the essential items that can aid in the construction and finishing of your amigurumi. These tools not only make the process more efficient but also ensure that your finished creations have a polished and professional look.

Moreover, joining amigurumi communities and seeking guidance from experienced crafters can greatly enhance your amigurumi journey. Online forums, social media groups, and local knitting or crochet clubs are excellent platforms to connect with fellow amigurumi enthusiasts. Sharing your progress, seeking advice, and learning from others can provide valuable insights and inspiration. Additionally, participating in amigurumi swaps or challenges can motivate you to explore new techniques and push your creative boundaries.

Lastly, it is important to approach your amigurumi journey with patience and a positive mindset. Amigurumi requires attention to detail and precision, which can sometimes be time-consuming

Understanding Amigurumi and Its Charm: Amigurumi is a Japanese art form that involves creating small, stuffed animals or objects using crochet or knitting techniques. The word "amigurumi" is derived from the Japanese words "ami," meaning crocheted or knitted, and "nuigurumi," meaning stuffed doll. This craft has gained popularity worldwide due to its unique and adorable designs.

One of the main reasons why amigurumi has captured the hearts of many is its charm. These handmade creations have a certain whimsical and cute appeal that is hard to resist. The small size of amigurumi makes them perfect for collecting or displaying on shelves, desks, or even as keychains. Their adorable features, such as big eyes, tiny limbs, and chubby bodies, make them incredibly endearing and appealing to people of all ages.

Amigurumi can be made using a variety of materials, but the most common ones are yarn and a crochet hook. The process involves creating individual pieces, such as the head, body, arms, and legs, and then stitching them together to form the final shape. The details, such as facial expressions, clothing, and accessories, are added using embroidery or other decorative techniques. This allows for endless possibilities in terms of design and customization.

The art of amigurumi requires patience, precision, and creativity. Each piece is meticulously crafted, with attention to detail given to every stitch and embellishment. The process of creating amigurumi can be both relaxing and rewarding, as it allows crafters to express their creativity and bring their imagination to life. It is a form of art that combines the technical skills of crochet or knitting with the artistic vision of the creator.

Amigurumi is not only a craft but also a form of self-expression. Crafters can create their own unique designs or replicate characters from their favorite movies, cartoons, or video games. This allows them to showcase their personality and interests through their creations. Additionally, amigurumi can be given as gifts to loved ones, making them even more special and meaningful.

The popularity of amigurumi has led to the formation of online communities and social media groups dedicated to this craft. These platforms provide a space for crafters to share their creations, exchange tips and techniques, and inspire each other. The sense of community and camaraderie among amigurumi enthusiasts is one of the reasons why this craft continues to thrive and evolve.

Gathering Your Crochet Materials and Tools:

Crocheting is a popular and enjoyable craft that allows you to create beautiful and intricate designs using yarn and a crochet hook. Before you can start crocheting, it's important to gather all the necessary materials and tools. This will ensure that you have everything you need to complete your crochet projects with ease and efficiency.

The first and most essential item you'll need is yarn. Yarn comes in a variety of colors, textures, and thicknesses, so it's important to choose the right type for your project. Consider the weight of the yarn, which refers to its thickness, as this will determine the size of your stitches and the overall look of your finished piece. You can find yarn at craft stores, online retailers, or even in your own stash if you're an experienced crocheter.

Next, you'll need a crochet hook. Crochet hooks come in different sizes, which correspond to the thickness of the yarn you're using. The size of the hook will affect the size of your stitches, so be sure to choose the appropriate hook for your project. Crochet hooks are typically made of metal, plastic, or wood, and each material has its own advantages and disadvantages. Experiment with different types of hooks to find the one that feels most comfortable in your hand.

In addition to yarn and a crochet hook, you'll also need a few other tools to complete your crochet projects. One essential tool is a pair of scissors, which you'll use to cut the yarn. It's important to have a sharp pair of scissors that can easily cut through the yarn without fraying or damaging it.

Another useful tool is a yarn needle or tapestry needle. This needle has a large eye and a blunt tip, making it perfect for weaving in loose ends and sewing pieces together. A yarn needle is especially handy when working on projects that require joining multiple pieces or adding embellishments.

If you're working on a more complex project or using a pattern, it can be helpful to have stitch markers. These small, removable markers are used to mark specific stitches or sections of your work, making it easier to keep track of your progress and follow the pattern accurately.

Finally, it's important to have a dedicated space for your crochet materials and tools. Consider investing in a crochet bag or storage container to keep everything organized and easily accessible. This will save you time and frustration when you're ready to start a new project or continue working on an existing one.

Basic Stitches and Techniques for Amigurumi: Amigurumi is the Japanese art of crocheting or knitting small stuffed animals or dolls. It has gained popularity worldwide due to its adorable and whimsical designs. If you are new to amigurumi, learning the basic stitches and techniques is essential to create your own cute and cuddly creations.

1. Slip Stitch: The slip stitch is the most basic stitch in amigurumi. It is used to join rounds or to move to a different part of your work. To make a slip stitch, insert your hook into the designated stitch, yarn over, and pull the yarn through both the stitch and the loop on your hook.

2. Single Crochet: The single crochet stitch is the foundation of amigurumi. It creates a tight and dense fabric, perfect for stuffing. To make a single crochet, insert your hook into the designated stitch, yarn over, and pull the yarn through the stitch. Yarn over again and pull through both loops on your hook.

3. Magic Ring: The magic ring technique is used to start crocheting in the round. It creates a tight and adjustable center for your amigurumi. To make a magic ring, hold the end of your yarn between your thumb and middle finger. Wrap the yarn around your index finger, creating a loop. Insert your hook into the loop, yarn over, and pull the yarn through. Then, chain one to secure the ring.

4. Increase: Increasing is used to add stitches and shape your amigurumi. It is usually done by making two single crochets in the same stitch. To increase, make a single crochet in the designated stitch, then make another single crochet in the same stitch.

5. Decrease: Decreasing is used to decrease the number of stitches and shape your amigurumi. It is usually done by combining two stitches into one. To decrease, insert your hook into the first stitch, yarn over, and pull the yarn through. Then, insert your hook into the next stitch, yarn over, and pull the yarn through. Yarn over again and pull through all three loops on your hook.

6. Invisible Decrease: The invisible decrease is a technique used to create a neater and less noticeable decrease. It is especially useful when working with light-colored yarn or when you want a more polished finish.

Reading and Following Amigurumi Patterns: Reading and following amigurumi patterns can be a fun and rewarding experience for crafters of all skill levels. Amigurumi, which is the Japanese art of crocheting or knitting small stuffed animals or toys, has gained popularity worldwide in recent years. Whether you are a beginner or an experienced crocheter, understanding how to read and follow amigurumi patterns is essential to creating beautiful and intricate designs.

The first step in reading an amigurumi pattern is to familiarize yourself with the abbreviations and symbols commonly used in these patterns. Amigurumi patterns often use abbreviations to represent different stitches and techniques. For example, "sc stands for single crochet, "inc" stands for increase, and "dec" stands for decrease. It is important to have a reference guide or chart handy to help you understand these abbreviations and symbols.

Once you are familiar with the abbreviations, the next step is to carefully read through the pattern instructions. Amigurumi patterns typically include a list of materials needed, such as the type and weight of yarn, the size of crochet hook, and any additional supplies like safety eyes or stuffing. Make sure you have all the necessary materials before you begin.

The pattern will then provide step-by-step instructions on how to create each part of the amigurumi, starting with the body or base. These instructions will often include the number of stitches to make, the type of stitch to use, and any increases or decreases needed to shape the piece. It is important to follow these instructions closely to ensure that your amigurumi turns out as intended.

In addition to the written instructions, amigurumi patterns may also include diagrams or charts to help visualize the construction process. These diagrams can be especially helpful for understanding complex stitch patterns or shaping techniques. Take the time to study these diagrams and refer to them as needed while working on your project.

As you work through the pattern, it is important to keep track of your progress. This can be done by using stitch markers or by simply counting your stitches after each row or round. This will help you stay organized and ensure that you are following the pattern correctly.

If you come across any difficulties or have questions while working on an amigurumi pattern, don't hesitate to seek help. There are many online communities and forums dedicated to amigurumi where you can ask for advice or clarification. Additionally, many pattern designers provide support and assistance through their websites or"

Ideas for Additional Food Amigurumi: Here are some ideas for additional food amigurumi that you can create:

1. Sushi Roll: Sushi rolls are a popular and visually appealing food item that would make a great addition to your amigurumi collection. You can create different types of sushi rolls such as California rolls, spicy tuna rolls, or even vegetarian rolls. Use different colors of yarn to represent the various ingredients like rice, seaweed, and fish or vegetables.

2. Cupcake: Cupcakes are a sweet treat that can be customized in many ways. You can create amigurumi cupcakes with different flavors and toppings. Use different colors of yarn to represent the cupcake base and frosting. Add small details like sprinkles or a cherry on top to make it more realistic.

3. Ice Cream Cone: Ice cream cones are a classic dessert that can be made in various flavors and combinations. Create amigurumi ice cream cones with different flavors like chocolate, vanilla, or strawberry. Use different colors of yarn to represent the ice cream scoops and add a cone-shaped base to complete the look.

4. Pizza Slice: Pizza is a beloved food item that can be made in countless variations. Create amigurumi pizza slices with different toppings like pepperoni, mushrooms, or olives. Use different colors of yarn to represent the crust, sauce, and cheese. You can even add small details like tiny mushrooms or pepperoni slices to make it more realistic.

5. Donut: Donuts are a popular breakfast treat that can be made in various flavors and shapes. Create amigurumi donuts with different flavors like chocolate, glazed, or strawberry. Use different colors of yarn to represent the icing and add small details like sprinkles or a drizzle of chocolate to make it more visually appealing.

6. Hamburger: Hamburgers are a classic fast food item that can be made with different ingredients and toppings. Create amigurumi hamburgers with a bun, patty, lettuce, tomato, and cheese. Use different colors of yarn to represent each ingredient and add small details like sesame seeds on the bun or a slice of pickle to make it more realistic.

7. Pancakes: Pancakes are a delicious breakfast option that can be made in various flavors and sizes. Create amigurumi pancakes with different toppings like syrup, butter, or fruits. Use different colors of yarn to represent the pancake stack and add small details like a dollop of whipped cream or a slice of

Tips for Designing Your Own Culinary Amigurumi: Designing your own culinary amigurumi can be a fun and creative way to express your love for both food and crochet. Whether you're a beginner or an experienced crocheter, there are a few tips that can help you create a unique and adorable culinary amigurumi.

Firstly, it's important to gather inspiration for your design. Look for pictures of your favorite food items or search for existing amigurumi patterns online. This will give you an idea of the shape, colors, and details you want to incorporate into your design. You can also take inspiration from real-life food items, such as fruits, vegetables, desserts, or even fast food.

Once you have your inspiration, it's time to choose the right yarn and crochet hook. Consider the size of your amigurumi and the level of detail you want to achieve. Thicker yarn and larger hooks will create a larger amigurumi with less detail, while thinner yarn and smaller hooks will result in a smaller amigurumi with more intricate details. Experiment with different yarn weights and hook sizes to find the perfect combination for your design.

Next, think about the construction of your amigurumi. Consider how you will create the different parts of your design, such as the body, limbs, and facial features. You can choose to crochet each part separately and then sew them together, or you can crochet them all in one piece. Keep in mind that crocheting each part separately will allow for more flexibility in shaping and positioning.

When it comes to adding details to your culinary amigurumi, there are several techniques you can use. Embroidery can be used to create facial features, such as eyes, mouth, and eyebrows. You can also use embroidery to add texture, such as seeds on a strawberry or sprinkles on a cupcake. Additionally, you can use felt or fabric to create additional details, such as a cherry on top of an ice cream cone or a lettuce leaf on a burger.

Color choice is another important aspect of designing your culinary amigurumi. Consider the colors of the food item you're trying to recreate and choose yarn colors that closely match. You can also experiment with different shades and tones to add depth and dimension to your design. Don't be afraid to get creative with your color choices and mix and match different colors to make your amigurumi truly unique.

Challenges in Creating Diverse Crochet Dishes: Creating diverse crochet dishes can be a challenging task due to several factors. One of the main challenges is finding inspiration and coming up with unique designs. Crochet dishes are not as common as other crochet items like blankets or scarves, so there is a limited pool of existing designs to draw inspiration from. This means that crocheters have to think outside the box and come up with their own original ideas.

Another challenge is selecting the right yarn and colors for the dish. Crochet dishes can be made using a variety of yarn weights and textures, and choosing the right one can greatly impact the final result. Additionally, selecting the right colors is crucial in creating diverse crochet dishes. Different color combinations can give a dish a completely different look and feel, so crocheters need to carefully consider their choices to achieve the desired diversity.

The size and shape of the dish also pose challenges. Crochet dishes can come in various shapes and sizes, from small bowls to large platters. Each shape requires a different crochet technique and pattern, which adds complexity to the creation process. Crocheters need to have a good understanding of different crochet stitches and techniques to successfully create diverse dishes.

Furthermore, the functionality of the dish is an important aspect to consider. Crochet dishes can be used for various purposes, such as serving food, holding small items, or simply as decorative pieces. Ensuring that the dish is functional and practical while still maintaining its aesthetic appeal can be a tricky balance to achieve.

Lastly, the finishing touches and details of the dish can make a significant difference in its overall appearance. Adding embellishments, such as buttons, beads, or embroidery, can enhance the diversity of the dish and make it stand out. However, incorporating these details requires precision and skill, as they need to be seamlessly integrated into the crochet work.

In conclusion, creating diverse crochet dishes is a challenging endeavor that requires creativity, attention to detail, and a good understanding of crochet techniques. From finding inspiration and selecting the right yarn and colors, to considering the size, shape, functionality, and finishing touches, every aspect plays a crucial role in achieving diversity in crochet dishes. Despite the challenges, the end result can be incredibly rewarding, as it allows crocheters to showcase their unique style and creativity in a functional and beautiful way.

Joining Online Communities and Challenges of Crochet Amigurumi: Joining online communities can be a great way to connect with fellow crochet enthusiasts and learn new techniques. One specific challenge that many crocheters face when it comes to online communities is the world of crochet amigurumi.

Crochet amigurumi refers to the art of creating small stuffed animals or dolls using crochet techniques. It has gained immense popularity in recent years, with countless patterns and designs available online. However, mastering the art of crochet amigurumi can be quite challenging, especially for beginners.

One of the main challenges of crochet amigurumi is understanding the intricate patterns and techniques involved. Unlike traditional crochet projects like scarves or blankets, amigurumi requires a different set of skills. It involves working in the round, using different stitch counts, and creating three-dimensional shapes. This can be overwhelming for beginners who are used to working in rows and creating flat pieces.

Another challenge of crochet amigurumi is achieving the right tension and gauge. Tension refers to the tightness or looseness of your stitches, and it plays a crucial role in creating amigurumi toys. If your tension is too tight, your stitches will be too small, resulting in a stiff and rigid toy. On the other hand, if your tension is too loose, your stitches will be too big, and the stuffing may show through. Achieving the perfect tension can take time and practice, and it can be frustrating for beginners.

Additionally, joining online communities for crochet amigurumi can be overwhelming due to the vast amount of information available. There are numerous websites, forums, and social media groups dedicated to amigurumi, each offering different patterns, tips, and techniques. It can be challenging to navigate through all this information and find reliable sources. Beginners may also feel intimidated by the advanced projects and intricate designs shared by experienced crocheters in these communities.

However, despite these challenges, joining online communities for crochet amigurumi can be incredibly rewarding. These communities provide a platform for crocheters to share their work, seek advice, and learn from each other. They offer a supportive and encouraging environment where beginners can ask questions and receive guidance from more experienced crocheters. Online communities also provide access to a wide range of patterns and tutorials, making it easier for beginners to find projects suited to their skill level.

Keeping Your Amigurumi Clean and Vibrant: Amigurumi, the adorable crocheted or knitted stuffed toys, have gained immense popularity in recent years. These cute little creatures bring joy and comfort to people of all ages. However, just like any other plush toy, amigurumi can accumulate dirt and lose their vibrancy over time. To ensure that your amigurumi remains clean and vibrant, it is important to follow a few simple steps.

First and foremost, it is essential to handle your amigurumi with clean hands. Oils and dirt from our hands can easily transfer onto the toy's surface, leading to a dull appearance. Before playing or handling your amigurumi, make sure to wash your hands thoroughly with soap and water. This will help prevent any unwanted dirt or oils from transferring onto the toy.

Regular cleaning is also crucial in maintaining the vibrancy of your amigurumi. Depending on the material used, you can either hand wash or machine wash your toy. For delicate amigurumi made from natural fibers such as cotton or wool, hand washing is recommended. Fill a basin with lukewarm water and add a mild detergent specifically designed for delicate fabrics. Gently submerge the amigurumi in the soapy water and lightly agitate it to remove any dirt or stains. Rinse the toy thoroughly with clean water to remove any soap residue. Squeeze out excess water, taking care not to wring or twist the toy, as this can damage its shape. Finally, lay the amigurumi flat on a clean towel and allow it to air dry completely.

If your amigurumi is made from synthetic fibers such as acrylic or polyester, machine washing may be an option. However, it is important to check the care instructions provided by the manufacturer before proceeding. Place the amigurumi in a mesh laundry bag to protect it from getting tangled or damaged during the wash cycle. Use a gentle or delicate cycle with cold water and a mild detergent. Once the wash cycle is complete, remove the amigurumi from the mesh bag and gently squeeze out excess water. Again, lay the toy flat on a clean towel and allow it to air dry completely.

In addition to regular cleaning, it is important to protect your amigurumi from excessive sunlight and dust. Prolonged exposure to direct sunlight can cause the colors to fade over time.

Storing and Displaying Your Crochet Items: Storing and displaying your crochet items is an essential aspect of maintaining their quality and showcasing your hard work. Whether you are a beginner or an experienced crocheter, it is important to have a system in place to keep your creations organized and easily accessible. This not only helps in preserving the integrity of your crochet items but also allows you to proudly display them in your home or gift them to others.

When it comes to storing your crochet items, there are a few key factors to consider. Firstly, it is crucial to keep your creations in a clean and dry environment to prevent any damage or deterioration. Moisture can lead to mold or mildew growth, which can ruin your crochet items. Therefore, it is advisable to store them in airtight containers or bags, preferably with moisture-absorbing packets to maintain optimal conditions.

Additionally, it is important to protect your crochet items from dust and dirt. You can achieve this by using garment bags or covers specifically designed for storing textiles. These covers not only shield your crochet items from external elements but also allow for easy visibility, making it convenient to locate specific pieces when needed.

Another aspect to consider is the organization of your crochet items. Depending on the size and quantity of your creations, you may want to categorize them by type, size, or color. This can be done by using dividers or separate containers within your storage space. By organizing your crochet items, you can easily find what you need without having to rummage through a cluttered pile.

In addition to proper storage, displaying your crochet items can add a touch of beauty and creativity to your living space. There are various ways to showcase your creations, depending on your personal style and the available space. One popular option is to use decorative hooks or hangers to hang your crochet items on walls or doors. This not only adds visual interest but also keeps your creations easily accessible and free from any potential damage.

If you have a larger collection of crochet items, you may consider creating a dedicated display area, such as a shelf or cabinet. This allows you to arrange your creations in an aesthetically pleasing manner, creating a focal point in your home. You can further enhance the display by incorporating other decorative elements, such as plants or artwork, to create a cohesive and visually appealing arrangement.

Furthermore, displaying your crochet items can also serve as a source of inspiration for your own future projects or for others who visit your home.

Repairing Wear and Tear in Amigurumi: Amigurumi, the Japanese art of crocheting or knitting small stuffed toys, has gained immense popularity in recent years. These adorable creations bring joy to both children and adults alike. However, with frequent use and handling, wear and tear can occur, causing the amigurumi to lose its charm and appeal. In such cases, it becomes necessary to repair the damage and restore the toy to its former glory.

One common issue that amigurumi enthusiasts face is unraveling or fraying of the yarn. This can happen due to the constant pulling and tugging that the toy undergoes during playtime. To repair this, you will need a crochet hook or a tapestry needle, depending on the severity of the damage. Start by carefully examining the affected area and identifying any loose or broken stitches. Gently unravel the damaged portion, making sure not to pull too hard and cause further damage. Once the damaged stitches have been removed, reattach the yarn by inserting the crochet hook or tapestry needle through the adjacent stitches and pulling the yarn through. Repeat this process until the damaged area has been fully repaired. To ensure a seamless finish, it is important to match the tension and stitch size of the surrounding area.

Another common issue that may arise is stuffing coming out of the amigurumi. This can occur when the toy is subjected to rough play or excessive squeezing. To fix this, you will need additional stuffing material and a sewing needle. Begin by carefully examining the damaged area and identifying any holes or openings. If the stuffing has completely come out, start by inserting the sewing needle through the opening and securing it to the surrounding stitches. Then, gradually fill the toy with the additional stuffing material, making sure to distribute it evenly. Once the toy is adequately stuffed, use the sewing needle to close the opening by stitching it back together. It is important to use small, discreet stitches to ensure that the repair is not noticeable.

In some cases, the amigurumi may have small accessories, such as buttons or beads, that have come loose or fallen off. To repair this, you will need a sewing needle and thread that matches the color of the accessory. Begin by carefully examining the toy and identifying any missing or loose accessories. If the accessory has fallen off completely, thread the sewing needle and insert it through the amigurumi at the desired location. Then, thread the accessory onto the needle and carefully sew it back onto the toy, making sure to secure.

MATERIALS & TOOLS

TO COMPLETE THE PATTERNS IN THIS BOOK, HERE IS A
LIST OF THE MATERIALS AND TOOLS YOU WILL NEED.

YARN

My go-to yarn for amigurumi is worsted weight acrylic. Acrylic yarn tends to hold its shape better, and this is key when making stuffed toys. Worsted weight is referred to as a level 4, or medium-weight yarn. Acrylic yarn is also very affordable and comes in a large variety of colors. Brands I like to use are Red Heart Super Saver, Lion Brand Vanna's Choice Yarn, and Caron Simply Soft. Choose your favorite brands and colors for the projects in this book!

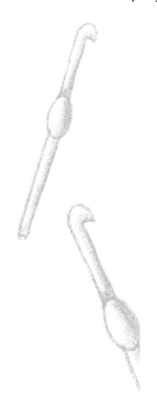

CROCHET HOOKS

Crochet hooks vary in size and can be made of aluminum, wood, or plastic. Some have ergonomic handles, which I prefer when crocheting amigurumi. Choose a hook that works and feels comfortable in your hand. You will only need two sizes for the projects in this book: F/3.75mm and G/4mm. Of course, you can use a smaller or larger hook, but your amigurumi may turn out smaller or bigger than mine if you do.

SAFETY EYES

Safety eyes come in many sizes and colors. We will use solid black safety eyes in two sizes: 6mm and 9mm. Safety eyes have a plastic or metal washer that attaches to the back of the eye once inserted into the crocheted piece. Make sure you have positioned the eyes exactly where you would like before attaching the backs, as they are impossible to remove once attached. Buttons, felt, or embroidered eyes are a great alternative to safety eyes.

NOTE: If you plan on giving the items you create to small children, I always recommend replacing the safety eyes with felt or embroidering them using yarn or thread.

FIBERFILL STUFFING

Polyester fiberfill is great for stuffing amigurumi. Make sure to add enough that your items will hold their shape, but not too much. Overstuffing will cause the stitches to stretch and the stuffing to show through.

YARN NEEDLE

Also called darning or tapestry needles, yarn needles have a blunt tip and a much bigger eye, which makes it super easy to thread yarn into. This needle is ideal for sewing pieces together or weaving in ends.

EMBROIDERY NEEDLE AND FLOSS

Much smaller than yarn needles, embroidery needles are used for adding the finer details, like mouths and small embellishments. Embroidery floss is great for adding those details. For thicker mouths use all 6 strands, and for thinner mouths use 3 strands. Do what you think looks best! For these projects we'll be using mostly black, white, and pink. Some projects may need a few more colors for things like sprinkles, so choose your favorite colors for those!

STITCH MARKERS

Stitch markers are a must when crocheting amigurumi! Because we will be crocheting in the round for these projects, you'll need a few of these to mark the end of each round. Safety pins also work great if you don't want to purchase markers.

SCISSORS

A sharp pair of scissors will come in handy when you need to trim yarn or embroidery floss or cut felt details.

STRAIGHT PINS

I love to use straight pins before I commit to sewing pieces together. Using pins helps with positioning items and allows your sewn pieces to be exactly where you want them.

FELT

A great way to add other facial features or small details is to use felt. Use embroidery floss or hot glue to add felt to the crocheted pieces.

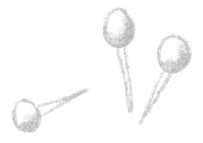

PIPE CLEANERS

Pipe cleaners (also known as chenille stems) are great for adding a little stability or bend to an item. Use them for the bendy straw on the juice box (this page), the popsicle stick (this page), or the stem on the wine glass (this page).

THICK AND THIN CARDBOARD

Cardboard can be very helpful for making pieces more flat and sturdy. I like to reuse cereal boxes for thin pieces of cardboard. For thicker cardboard I like to reuse corrugated shipping boxes. Be sure to not get items that contain cardboard wet. If cleaning is required, I recommend spot cleaning and allowing the piece to air-dry.

HOT GLUE GUN

Use a hot glue gun for adding felt details or other crocheted pieces in place. This works great if you don't want to sew them in place.

ABBREVIATIONS

BLO

Back Loops Only

BO

Bobble

CH

Chain

DC

Double Crochet

DC2TOG

Double Crochet 2 Together

DEC

Decrease

FLO

Front Loops Only

HDC

Half Double Crochet

INC

Increase

INV DEC

Invisible Decrease

R

Round or Row

SC

Single Crochet

SK

Skip

SL ST

Slip Stitch

ST/S

Stitch/es

TR

Treble Crochet

*Repeat steps between asterisks as many times as stated

() The number inside the parentheses indicates how many stitches you will have at the end of each round

STITCHES & TECHNIQUES

The following are the stitches and techniques used throughout the projects in this book. The patterns in this book are written using US crochet terminology.

Each pattern is worked in continuous rounds like a spiral. Use a stitch marker to mark the end of each round.

GAUGE

While gauge is an important step in crocheting, for amigurumi it isn't too important. Everyone holds the yarn differently, so your tension may be different than mine. Make sure your tension is even throughout and that your stitches aren't too loose, allowing the fiberfill to show through. Keep in mind that using a smaller or larger hook size and different yarn will change the size of your toys. Measurements for each project are given and are a rough estimate of what the finished sizes will be.

RIGHT SIDE/WRONG SIDE OF WORK

When working your pieces, you'll notice that one side is always facing you. This side is considered the "right" side of the work. The side facing away from you is the "wrong" side, or the back side of the work. One way to decipher which side is which is to simply look at the side facing you and look for the "V." *(photo 1)* If you turn your work over to the back side, you'll notice that there is a horizontal bar between each row of "Vs." *(photo 2)* There is no wrong or right here; simply choose a side you think looks best!

YARN OVER (YO)

To yarn over, simply take your hook and grab hold of the yarn.

The yarn will be going over your hook, and you can proceed to pull it through the loop or stitch.

MAGiC RiNG (MR)

Also known as an adjustable ring, I prefer this method because it closes up the piece more and doesn't leave a small hole at the top.

TO MAKE A MAGIC RiNG:

1 Make a loop and place the working yarn on top of the loose tail. *(photo 1)*

2 Insert hook into loop, grabbing the working yarn with the hook. Pull through the loop. *(photos 2+3)*

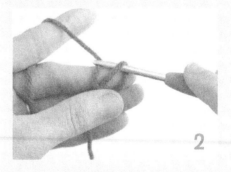

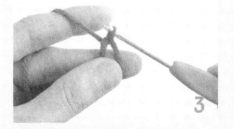

3 Yarn over and pull hook through loop. This is considered a "Ch 1." *(photo 4)*

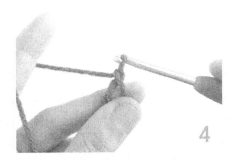

This next step is where you will start making single crochets into the magic ring.

4 Insert the hook back into the ring. Make sure to go under both strands. *(photo 5)*

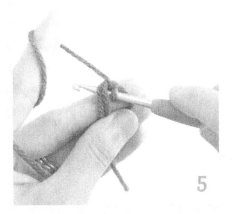

5 Yarn over and pull hook through ring. 2 loops will be on the hook. *(photos 6+7)*

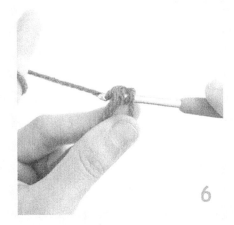

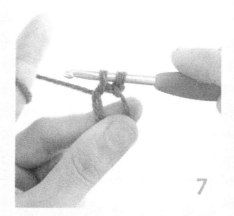

7

6 Yarn over and pull through both loops. 1 loop will remain on the hook. This completes your first single crochet. *(photo 8)*

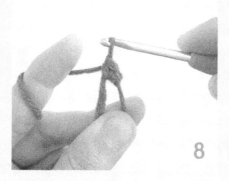

8

7 Repeat steps 4–6 as many times as the pattern states. Most patterns state 6 single crochet (6 sc) in the magic ring. *(photo 9)*

9

8 Grab the loose tail and pull to close the ring. You now have a completed magic ring. *(photo 10)*

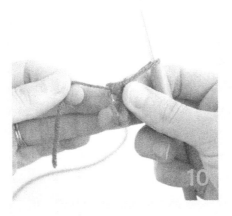

To begin the next round, place the next stitch into the first single crochet made in step 6. *(photo 11)*

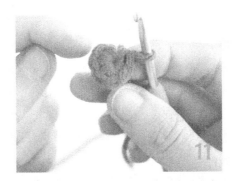

SINGLE CROCHET (SC)

1 Insert hook into stitch and yarn over. *(photos 1+2)*

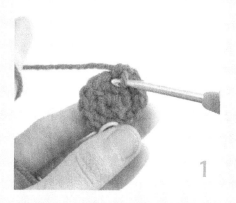

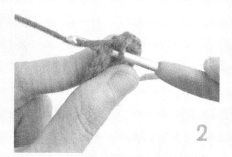

2 Pull hook through stitch. There will be 2 loops on your hook. *(photo 3)*

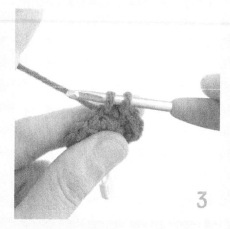

3 Yarn over again and pull through both loops. 1 loop will remain on the hook. *(photos 4+5)*

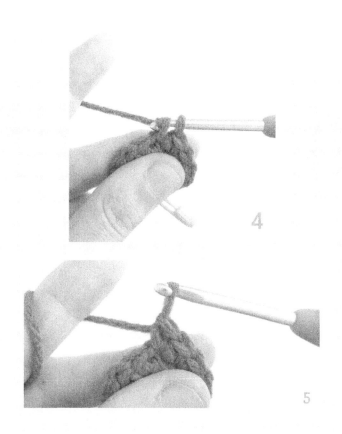

4

5

INCREASE (INC)

An increase is used to expand your piece and make it bigger. To increase simply place 2 single crochet into 1 stitch. If you look at the photo, you'll see two "Vs" in one stitch. *(photo 1)* This is an increase.

HALF DOUBLE CROCHET (HDC)

1 Yarn over and insert hook into stitch. *(photos 1+2)*

2 Yarn over and pull hook through stitch. 3 loops will remain on the hook. *(photo 3)*

3 Yarn over and pull through all 3 loops. 1 loop will remain on the hook. *(photos 4+5)*

DOUBLE CROCHET (DC)

1 Yarn over and insert hook into stitch. *(photos 1+2)*

2 Yarn over and pull hook through stitch. 3 loops will remain on the hook.
(photo 3)

3 Yarn over and pull through 2 loops. 2 loops will remain on the hook. *(photos 4+5)*

4 Yarn over for a final time and pull hook through remaining 2 loops. 1 loop will remain on the hook. *(photo 6)*

TREBLE CROCHET (TR)

1 Yarn over two times so that 3 loops are on the hook. *(photo 1)*

2 Insert hook into stitch and yarn over. *(photo 2)*

3 Pull hook through stitch. There will be 4 loops on your hook. *(photo 3)*

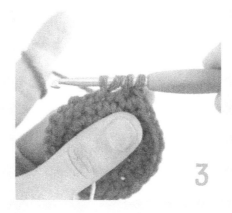

4 Yarn over and pull through 2 loops. 3 loops will remain on the hook. *(photos 4+5)*

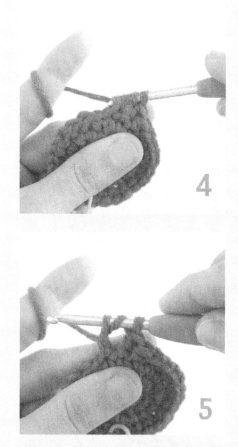

5 Yarn over again and pull through another 2 loops. 2 loops will remain on the hook. *(photos 6+7)*

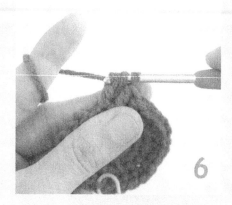

6 Yarn over for a final time and pull through the remaining 2 loops. 1 loop will remain on the hook. *(photo 8)*

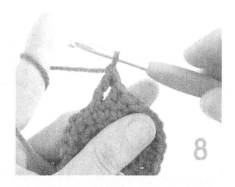

FRONT AND BACK LOOPS ONLY (FLO OR BLO)

Some of the patterns in this book use this technique. When holding your work, you'll see from the top that the stitches looks like a sideways "V." The side closest to you is the front loop *(photo 1)*, and the one behind is the back loop. *(photo 2)* When the pattern states to crochet "In FLO," work the stitches in the front loops only. *(photo 3)* When the pattern states to crochet "In BLO," insert hook into the center of the V and work the stitches in the back loops. *(photo 4)*

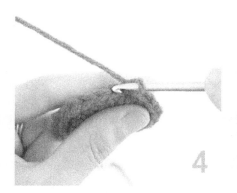

4

INVISIBLE DECREASE (INV DEC)

This is my favorite way to decrease amigurumi. A normal decrease tends to add a little bulk to the finished piece, while an invisible decrease is nearly impossible to spot.

TO INVISIBLE DECREASE:

1 Insert the hook into the FRONT loops only of the next two stitches. There will be 3 loops on your hook. *(photo 1)*

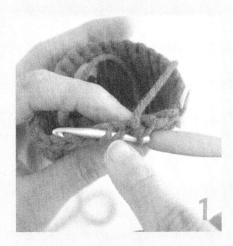

2 Yarn over and pull hook through the 2 front loops. 2 loops will remain on the hook. *(photos 2+3)*

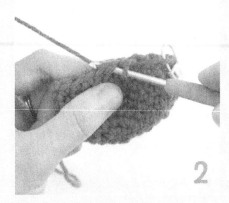

3 Yarn over again and pull through the 2 remaining loops. 1 loop will remain on the hook. *(photo 4)*

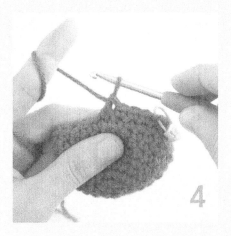

REGULAR DECREASE (DEC)

A couple patterns in this book use this technique for decreasing. This technique is used mainly when working flat pieces, not in the round.

1 Insert the hook into the next stitch. Yarn over and pull hook through. There will be 2 loops on your hook. *(photos 1+2)*

2 Insert the hook into the next stitch. Yarn over and pull hook through. There will be 3 loops on your hook. *(photos 3+4)*

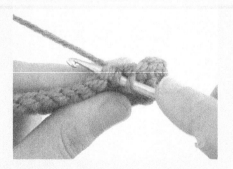

3 Yarn over for the last time and pull through all 3 loops. 1 loop will remain on your hook. *(photos 5+6)*

DOUBLE CROCHET 2 TOGETHER (DC2TOG)

1 Yarn over and insert hook into stitch. *(photos 1+2)*

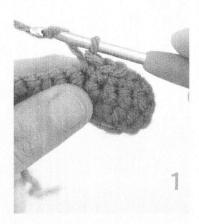

2 Yarn over and pull hook through stitch. There will be 3 loops on your hook. *(photo 3)*

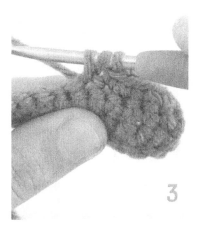

3 Yarn over again and pull through the first 2 loops. 2 loops will remain on the hook. *(photos 4+5)*

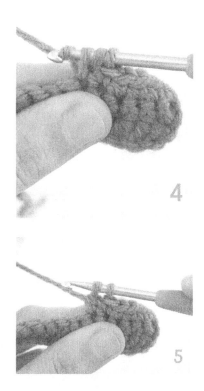

4 Yarn over and insert hook into the next stitch. *(photos 6+7)*

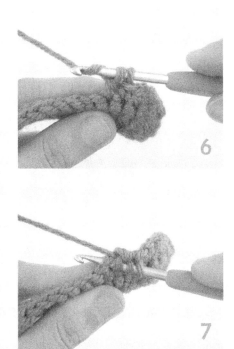

5 Yarn over and pull hook through stitch. There will be 4 loops on your hook. *(photo 8)*

6 Yarn over and pull through the first 2 loops again. 3 loops will remain on the hook. *(photo 9)*

7 Yarn over for the last time and pull through all 3 loops. 1 loop will remain on your hook. *(photo 10)*

BOBBLE STITCH (BO)

1 Yarn over and insert hook into stitch. *(photos 1+2)*

2 Yarn over and pull hook through stitch. There will be 3 loops on your hook. *(photo 3)*

3 Yarn over and pull through the first 2 loops. 2 loops will remain on the hook. *(photos 4+5)*

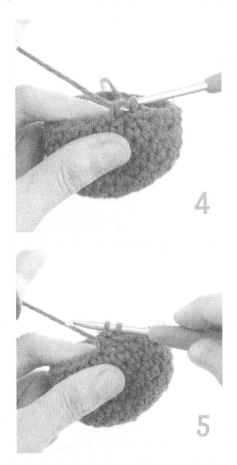

4 Repeat steps 1–3 a total of four more times, inserting the hook into the same stitch, until there are 6 loops on your hook. *(photo 6)*

5 Yarn over and pull through all loops on hook. 1 loop will remain on your hook. *(photos 7+8)*

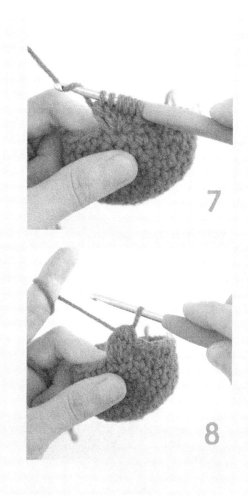

SLIP KNOT

1 Make a loop and place the loose tail on top of the working yarn. *(photo 1)*

2 Insert hook into loop and grab the loose tail. *(photos 2+3)*

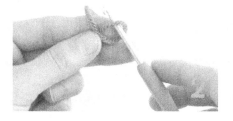

3 Pull the loose tail through the loop.

4 Holding both tails, pull to tighten the slip knot on the hook. *(photo 4)*

CHAIN (CH)

1 After you have made a slip knot, simply take the working yarn and yarn over. *(photo 1)*

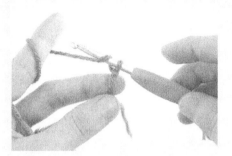

2 Pull hook through the slip knot. This is your first chain stitch. Repeat as many times as the pattern states. *(photos 2+3)*

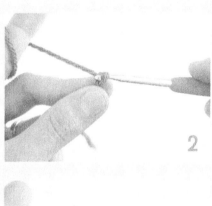

2

SLIP STITCH (SL ST)

1 Insert hook into stitch or chain and yarn over. *(photos 1+2)*

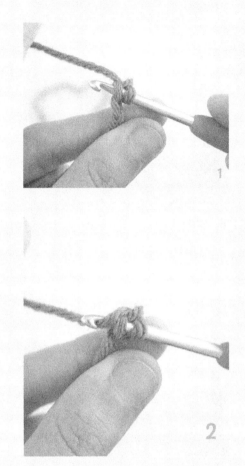

2 Pull hook through stitch or chain. There will be 2 loops on your hook. *(photo 3)*

3 Pull hook through the first loop. 1 loop will remain on the hook. *(photo 4)*

4

CLEAN COLOR CHANGING

1 When working the last stitch of the old color, do the typical single crochet until there are 2 loops left on the hook. *(photo 1)*

2 Use the new color to yarn over and complete the stitch. *(photos 2+3)*

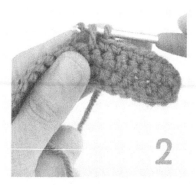

3 Sl st into the next stitch with the new color. *(photo 4)* This will count as a stitch.

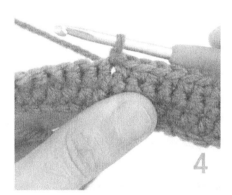

4 Continue to crochet as normal with the new color. *(photo 5)*

Trim the tail of the old color. Tie the tails from both colors together to secure the color change.

STAGGERED INCREASES AND DECREASES

You'll notice some of the designs in this book have patterns that show a staggered increase and decrease. Normally when you crochet a circle, it looks more like a hexagon as you build up the rounds. In order to form a "perfect" circle, the increases and decreases need to be alternated, but only on the even rounds.

The pattern will look something like this:

R3 *Sc 1, inc* 6 times. **(18 sts)**

R4 *Inc, sc 2* 6 times. **(24 sts)**

R5 *Sc 3, inc* 6 times. **(30 sts)**

R6 *Inc, sc 4* 6 times. **(36 sts)**

Notice the increase happens before the individual single crochets on the even rounds. *(photos 1+2)* The stitch count will be the same as it would be if you did not stagger the increases. The decreases will look the same, just with the invisible decrease coming before the single crochets.

ADDING A MOUTH

Thread your sewing needle with a length of embroidery floss about 5 to 6 inches long.

1 Bring the needle from inside the piece to the outside, near the safety eye on your left. *(photos 1+2)*

2 Go across to the right side and insert the needle into the piece. Don't pull the needle all the way through. *(photo 3)*

3 Hold the thread in a smile shape and bring the needle up through the center, one round down. *(photos 4+5)*

4 Pull the thread down to make a "V" shape. *(photo 6)*

6

5 Insert the needle close to the spot where it first came out. Bring the needle around the main piece of floss, making the smile, and then enter back into the piece. *(photo 7)*

6 Pull the thread through and make a knot to secure the floss. *(photo 8)*

8

MELTiNG THE BACKS OF SAFETY EYES

I know what you're thinking…melting safety eyes!? Hear me out! Some of the amigurumi patterns in this book are flat pieces, such as slices of toast or chips. When adding safety eyes to flat pieces, the post of the safety eye will poke through to the other side. *(photo 1)* It doesn't bother me much, but sometimes I like a clean finish all around. A technique I've learned is to use a lighter to soften the posts so you can make them flush with the crocheted piece. This way you can't see the safety eye poking through the other side.

1

Use extreme caution with this technique and only under adult supervision! To do this technique, fold the crocheted work away from the safety eye. Make sure the safety backing is attached. Take a lighter and carefully warm up the post and let it cool slightly before touching. Press the post flat. You'll have to repeat warming up the post a few times before it will be completely flat. *(photo 2)*

2

CLOSING UP YOUR PIECE

I like using this closing technique because it gives the piece a more finished look and the closure is nearly invisible.

1. When you've reached the end of the piece, cut the yarn and leave a tail for sewing. Pull the yarn tail through the loop on the hook and pull to secure. *(photo 1)*

2. Thread the yarn tail onto the needle. Insert the needle into the front loop of the first stitch, working from the center to the outside. Pull the needle through. Continue going through the front loops of the remaining stitches. *(photo 2)*

3. Once you have reached the end, pull the yarn tail and the hole will close. *(photo 3)*

4 Insert the needle into the center of the hole and bring out on the side of the piece. Secure with a knot, trim the tail, and hide inside piece. *(photos 4–6)*

MATERIALS

Worsted weight/4-ply yarn:
• Lime green
• Olive green
• Brown
• Tan

Size G/4mm crochet hook

1 pair of 9mm safety eyes for the toast

1 pair of 6mm safety eyes for the avocado

Black and white embroidery floss

Small embroidery needle

Fiberfill stuffing

Yarn needle

Stitch marker

Scissors

Thin cardboard

ABBREVIATIONS

CH   Chain

DC   Double Crochet

HDC   Half Double Crochet

INC	Increase
R	Round or Row
SC	Single Crochet
SL ST	Slip Stitch
ST/S	Stitch/es
TR	Treble Crochet

FINISHED MEASUREMENTS

AVOCADO TOAST

approx. 3.5 inches wide by 4 inches tall

AVOCADO

approx. 3.75 inches wide by 3.25 inches tall

Since the toast will be flat, the posts of the safety eyes will stick out the back. This can TOTALLY be left as is! But if you'd like them to be flush, use my trick to melt the backs (see Melting the Backs of Safety Eyes, this page). Make sure to fold your work away from the safety eyes, and use caution so the work doesn't catch. Adult supervision is required. Do this at your own risk!

AVOCADO

Using *lime green yarn,*

R1   6 sc in magic ring. **(6 sts)**

R2   Inc in each st around. **(12 sts)**

R3   *Sc 1, inc* 6 times. **(18 sts)**

R4   *Inc, sc 2* 6 times. **(24 sts)**

R5   *Sc 3, inc* 6 times. **(30 sts)**

This next round will build up the avocado.

R6   Sc 2, hdc dc, 2 dc, dc hdc, sc 3, hdc dc, dc hdc, sc 2, 2 hdc, 2 hdc, sc 2, hdc dc, 2 dc, dc hdc, sc 3, hdc dc, dc hdc, sc 3, 2 hdc, 2 hdc, sc 1. **(44 sts)** *(photos 1+2)*

1

2

R7 Sc 44.

Fasten off and leave a tail for sewing.

Add the 9mm safety eyes, placing them between rounds 3 and 4. Make sure to not attach the eye backing just yet. Sew on the mouth. With white and black embroidery floss, stitch "salt and pepper" in various places. *(photo 3)*

3

TOAST

MAKE 2

Using *tan yarn*, Ch 16.

R1 Starting in the 2nd ch from hook sc across. **(15 sts)** Ch 1 and turn.

R2-15 Sc 15. Ch 1 and turn.

This next row will form the top humps of the bread.

6   Sc hdc, hdc dc, 2 dc, 2 dc, 2 dc, dc hdc, hdc sc, sl st, sc hdc, hdc dc, 2 dc, 2 dc, 2 dc, dc hdc, hdc sc. **(29 sts)** *(photo 4)*

Change to *brown yarn,*

7   Sc around entire edge of the bread by sc 14, inc in corner, sc 13, inc in corner, sc 14, then sc 29 across top. **(74 sts)** *(photos 5+6)*

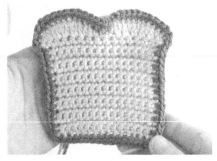

Fasten off and leave a brown tail for sewing (just on one piece of toast). Weave in all other ends.

TO ASSEMBLE THE AVOCADO TOAST

First, place the avocado on top of one slice of toast. Line up the safety eyes so they are between rounds 7 and 8 (counting from the bottom up), about 3 stitches apart. *(photos 7+8)* Attach the safety backings. Next, with the yarn needle, sew the avocado to the toast. Make sure to weave the needle through the stitches from R7 of the avocado and not over them. This will give the avocado a clean finish. *(photo 9)* Next, line up the two pieces of toast and, with the brown tail, sew the crusts together. Weave the yarn needle through the stitches from R17 and not over them *(photos 10–13)* Secure and hide ends. *(photo 14)*

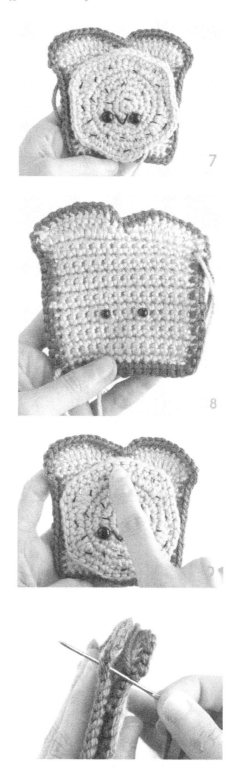

PIT

Using *brown yarn*,

R1   6 sc in magic ring. **(6 sts)**

R2   Inc in each st around. **(12 sts)**

R3   *Sc 1, inc* 6 times. **(18 sts)**

R4   *Inc, sc 2* 6 times. **(24 sts)**

R5   Sc 24.

Fasten off and leave a tail for sewing. Add the 6mm safety eyes, placing them between rounds 2 and 3, about 3 stitches apart. Sew on the mouth. *(photo 15)* Set aside.

15

AVOCADO

Using *lime green yarn*,

R1   6 sc in magic ring. **(6 sts)**

R2   Inc in each st around. **(12 sts)**

R3   *Sc 1, inc* 6 times. **(18 sts)**

R4   *Inc, sc 2* 6 times. **(24 sts)**

R5   *Sc 3, inc* 6 times. **(30 sts)**

R6   *Inc, sc 4* 6 times. **(36 sts)**

This next round will build up the avocado.

R7   Sc 13, 2 hdc, 2 dc, dc tr, 2 tr, 2 tr, 2 tr, 2 tr, tr dc, 2 dc, 2 hdc, sc 13. **(46 sts)** *(photos 16–19)*

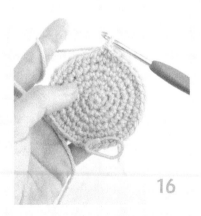

16

17

18

19

Fasten off and leave a tail for sewing.

With a yarn needle, sew the pit to the avocado. Make sure to line the pit up with R4 of the avocado. *(photo 20)* Weave the needle through the stitches from R3 and 4 and not over them. *(photos 21–24)* Before closing piece, add fiberfill to the pit. Secure and trim tail.

20

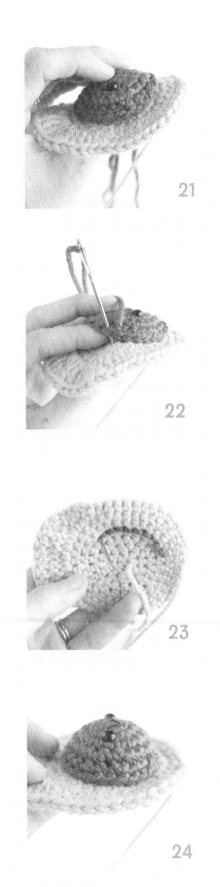

21

22

23

24

Trace the outline of the avocado on thin cardboard and cut it out. Set aside.

AVOCADO SKIN

Using *olive green yarn*,

R1   6 sc in magic ring. **(6 sts)**

R2   Inc in each st around. **(12 sts)**

R3   *Sc 1, inc* 6 times. **(18 sts)**

R4   *Inc, sc 2* 6 times. **(24 sts)**

R5   *Sc 3, inc* 6 times. **(30 sts)**

R6   *Inc, sc 4* 6 times. **(36 sts)**

R7   *Sc 5, inc* 6 times. **(42 sts)**

R8   *Sc 20, inc* 2 times. **(44 sts)**

R9   *Sc 21, inc* 2 times. **(46 sts)**

R1
0   Sc 46.

Fasten off and weave in the ends. *(photo 25)*

With a yarn needle, sew the avocado to the skin. Weave the needle through the back loops from R10 of the avocado skin and R7 of the avocado. *(photo 26–28)* Make sure to go through the stitches, and not over them, to create a clean finish around the avocado. *(photo 29)* At the halfway point insert the cardboard piece. *(photo 30)* Add fiberfill, making sure to not overstuff. Secure and hide the tail. *(photos 31+32)*

28

29

30

31

32

MATERIALS

Worsted weight/4-ply yarn:
• Maroon, red, cream for bacon
• White, yellow for eggs
• Tan, brown for toast

Size F/3.75mm crochet hook

3 pairs of 6mm safety eyes

Black embroidery floss

Small embroidery needle

Fiberfill stuffing

Yarn needle

Stitch marker

Scissors

Optional: pink felt and thread for cheeks

ABBREVIATIONS

Chain

Double Crochet 2 Together

Double Crochet

Decrease

Half Double Crochet

INC	Increase
R	Round or Row
SC	Single Crochet
ST/S	Stitch/es

FINISHED MEASUREMENTS

BACON

approx. 2 inches wide by 4 inches tall

EGG

approx. 3.25 inches wide by 0.75 inches tall

TOAST

approx. 3.5 inches wide by 4 inches tall

Since the bacon and toast will lay flat, the posts of the safety eyes will stick out the back. This can TOTALLY be left as is! But if you'd like them to be flush, use my trick to melt the backs (see Melting the Backs of Safety Eyes, this page). Make sure to fold your work away from the safety eyes and use caution so the work doesn't catch. Adult supervision is required. Do this at your own risk!

BACON

MAKE 2

Using **maroon yarn,** Ch 20.

The stitches for row 1 will be placed in the "bumps" behind the chain. *(photo 1)*

R1   Starting in the 2nd ch from hook hdc in the next 4 sts, dc2tog, hdc in the next 3 sts, 2 hdc in one st, hdc in the next 3 sts, dc2tog, hdc in the next 4 sts. **(18 sts)** *(photos 2–4)*

2

4

Change to *red yarn*, Ch 1 and turn.

R2   Sc 3, dec, sc 3, inc, sc 3, dec, sc 4. **(17 sts)** *(photo 5)*

5

Change to *cream yarn*, Ch 1 and turn.

R3   Sc 3, dec, sc 3, inc, sc 3, dec, sc 3. **(16 sts)** *(photo 6)*

Change to *maroon yarn,* Ch 1 and turn.

R4   Hdc in the next 3 sts, dc2tog, hdc in the next 2 sts, 2 hdc in one st, hdc in the next 3 sts, dc2tog, hdc in the next 3 sts. **(15 sts)** *(photo 7)*

Fasten off and leave a tail for sewing. Add the safety eyes, placing one between rows 1 and 2, about 5 stitches from the edge. Place the second eye between rows 3 and 4. Sew on the mouth. *(photos 8+9)* Only add eyes and mouth to one slice.

TO ASSEMBLE THE BACON

Line up both pieces and weave the yarn needle through row 4 of both pieces. *(photos 10+11)* Make sure to go through the stitches and not over them. *(photos 12+13)* Secure and hide the tail. *(photo 14)*

EGG

YOLK

Using *yellow yarn*,

R1 6 sc in magic ring. **(6 sts)**

R2 Inc in each st around. **(12 sts)**

R3 *Sc 1, inc* 6 times. **(18 sts)**

R4 Sc 18.

Fasten off and leave a tail for sewing. Add the safety eyes, placing them between rounds 2 and 3, about 3 stitches apart. Sew on the mouth. *(photo 15)* Set aside.

15

EGG WHiTE

Using *yellow yarn*,

R1   6 sc in magic ring. **(6 sts)**

R2   Inc in each st around. **(12 sts)**

R3   *Sc 1, inc* 6 times. **(18 sts)**

Change to   ,

R4   *Inc, sc 2* 6 times. **(24 sts)**

This next round will build up the wavy part of the egg white.

R5   Sc 4, sc hdc, hdc dc, 2 dc, dc hdc, hdc sc, sc 2, hdc dc, 2 dc, dc hdc, sc 3, sc hdc, 2 hdc, hdc sc, sc, hdc dc, dc hdc, sc. **(37 sts)** *(photo 16)*

16

R6   Sc 37.

Fasten off and weave in the ends.

TO ASSEMBLE THE EGG

With the tail left over from the egg yolk, weave the yarn needle between R4 of the egg yolk and R3 of the egg white where the yellow part is. Add fiberfill before closing. Secure and hide the tail.
(photos 17+18)

17

18

TOAST

Using *tan yarn*, Ch 2.

R1   In 2nd ch from hook inc. **(2 sts)** Ch 1 and turn.

R2   Inc, sc 1. **(3 sts)** Ch 1 and turn.

R3   Sc 2, inc. **(4 sts)** Ch 1 and turn.

R4   Sc 4. Ch 1 and turn.

R5   Sc 2, inc in the next 2 sts. **(6 sts)** Ch 1 and turn.

R6   Inc, sc 5. **(7 sts)** Ch 1 and turn.

R7   Sc 7. Ch 1 and turn.

R8   Inc in the next 2 sts, sc 5. **(9 sts)** Ch 1 and turn.

R9   Sc 9. Ch 1 and turn.

R10   Inc, sc 8. **(10 sts)** Ch 1 and turn.

R11   Sc 9, inc. **(11 sts)** Ch 1 and turn.

R12   Sc 11. Ch 1 and turn.

R13   Sc 10, inc. **(12 sts)** Ch 1 and turn.

R14   Sc 12. Ch 1 and turn.

R1

5 Sc 11, inc. **(13 sts)** Ch 1 and turn.

R1

6 Inc, sc 12. **(14 sts)** Ch 1 and turn.

R1

7 Sc 13, inc. **(15 sts)** Ch 1 and turn.

R1

8 Sc 15. Ch 1 and turn.

R1

9 Sc 14, inc. **(16 sts)**

Change to *brown yarn,* Ch 1 and turn.

R2

0 Sc 15, inc in last st (the corner space), then sc 18 along the side. **(35 sts)** *(photos 19+20)* Fasten off and leave a long tail for sewing. On one slice of bread, leave one long tan and one long brown tail. Weave in remaining tails. *(photo 21)*

Add the safety eyes, placing them between rows 5 and 6 (counting up from the bottom), about 2 stitches apart. Sew on the mouth. Add felt cheeks. *(photo 22)*

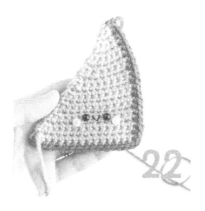

TO ASSEMBLE THE TOAST

With the brown tail, sew the crust together first. Weave the yarn needle through the stitches from R20, along the bottom and side. *(photos 23+24)* Make sure to weave through the stitches, not over, to create a clean finish. *(photo 25)* Then take the tan tail and sew the center of the bread together. Weave the yarn needle under, then over the sides. *(photos 26–29)* Secure and hide tails. *(photo 30)*

24

26

28

29

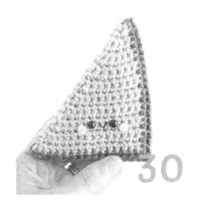

30

MATERIALS

Worsted weight/4-ply yarn:
- Tan
- White
- Pink
- Red
- Yellow

Size F/3.75mm crochet hook

1 pair of 6mm safety eyes

Black and dark green embroidery floss

Small embroidery needle

Fiberfill stuffing

Yarn needle

Stitch marker

Scissors

Optional: straight pins to help with assembling pieces

ABBREVIATIONS

DC	Double Crochet
HDC	Half Double Crochet
INC	Increase
INV DEC	Invisible Decrease

R   Round or Row

ST/S   Stitch/es

TR   Treble Crochet

SC   Single Crochet

FINISHED MEASUREMENTS

EGGS BENEDICT

approx. 3 inches wide by 2.25 inches tall

Using   ,

R1   6 sc in magic ring. **(6 sts)**

R2   Inc in each st around. **(12 sts)**

R3   *Sc 1, inc* 6 times. **(18 sts)**

R4   *Inc, sc 2* 6 times. **(24 sts)**

R5   *Sc 3, inc* 6 times. **(30 sts)**

R6   *Inc, sc 4* 6 times. **(36 sts)**

R7   *Sc 5, inc* 6 times. **(42 sts)**

R8+9   Sc 42.

Add the safety eyes, placing them between rounds 7 and 8, about 3 stitches apart. Using black embroidery floss, sew on mouth.

R10   *Sc 5, inv dec* 6 times. **(36 sts)**

R11   *Inv dec, sc 4* 6 times. **(30 sts)**

R12   *Sc 3, inv dec* 6 times. **(24 sts)**

R13   *Inv dec, sc 2* 6 times. **(18 sts)**

Begin adding fiberfill and continue as you close piece. Make sure to not overstuff.

R1

4   *Sc 1, inv dec* 6 times. **(12 sts)**

R1

5   Inv dec around 6 times. **(6 sts)**

Fasten off and leave a tail for closing the piece. Save the tail to sew the egg to the ham piece later. *(photo 1)*

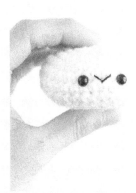

1

Using *yellow yarn*,

R1   6 sc in magic ring. **(6 sts)**

R2   Inc in each st around. **(12 sts)**

R3   *Sc 1, inc* 6 times. **(18 sts)**

R4   *Inc, sc 2* 6 times. **(24 sts)**

R5   *Sc 3, inc* 6 times. **(30 sts)**

This next row will form the drips.

R6   Sc, sc hdc, hdc dc, dc hdc, hdc sc, sc 3, hdc dc, dc hdc, sc 2, hdc dc, dc hdc, sc 4, hdc dc, dc tr, 2 tr, tr dc, dc hdc, sc 3, hdc dc, dc hdc, sc 2. **(45 sts)**

Fasten off and leave a tail for sewing. *(photo 2)*

2

With dark green embroidery floss, stitch lines in various places for the "parsley." *(photo 3)* Pin the sauce on top of the egg. *(photo 4)* With a yarn needle, sew the hollandaise sauce to the top of the egg. Weave the yarn needle through the stitches of **R6,** not over them, to create a clean finish. *(photo 5)* Secure and hide the tail. *(photo 6)*

3

4

5

6

Using *pink yarn*,

R1   6 sc in magic ring. **(6 sts)**

R2   Inc in each st around. **(12 sts)**

R3   *Sc 1, inc* 6 times. **(18 sts)**

R4   *Inc, sc 2* 6 times. **(24 sts)**

R5   *Sc 3, inc* 6 times. **(30 sts)**

R6   *Inc, sc 4* 6 times. **(36 sts)**

Change to *red yarn*,

R7   Sc 36.

Fasten off and leave a pink tail. Save the tail for sewing to the muffin piece later. Weave in all other ends. *(photo 7)*

7

With a yarn needle and the white tail from egg, sew the egg on top of the ham piece. *(photos 8–10)* Secure and hide the tail.

8

9

10

TOP PiECE

Using *tan yarn*,

R1   6 sc in magic ring. **(6 sts)**

R2   Inc in each st around. **(12 sts)**

R3   *Sc 1, inc* 6 times. **(18 sts)**

R4   *Inc, sc 2* 6 times. **(24 sts)**

R5   *Sc 3, inc* 6 times. **(30 sts)**

R6   *Inc, sc 4* 6 times. **(36 sts)**

R7   *Sc 5, inc* 6 times. **(42 sts)**

Fasten off and leave a tail for sewing. *(photo 11)*

11

With a yarn needle and the pink tail from the ham, sew the egg and ham to the top of the muffin piece. Weave the needle between the stitches of R5 and 6 of the ham piece. *(photos 12–16)* Secure with a knot and trim the tail.

12

13

14

15

16

BOTTOM PIECE

Using *tan yarn*,

R1   6 sc in magic ring. **(6 sts)**

R2   Inc in each st around. **(12 sts)**

R3   *Sc 1, inc* 6 times. **(18 sts)**

R4   *Inc, sc 2* 6 times. **(24 sts)**

R5   *Sc 3, inc* 6 times. **(30 sts)**

R6   *Inc, sc 4* 6 times. **(36 sts)**

R7   *Sc 5, inc* 6 times. **(42 sts)**

R8+9   Sc 42.

Fasten off and weave in the ends. *(photo 17)*

17

With a yarn needle, sew the top piece to the bottom piece. Weave the needle through the back loops of R9 on the bottom piece and the stitches of R7 on the top piece. *(photos 18+19)* Make sure to go through the stitches, not over them, to create a clean finish on the english muffin. *(photos 20+21)* Before closing the piece, add fiberfill, making sure to not overstuff. Secure and hide the tail.

19

20

21

MATERIALS

Worsted weight/4 ply yarn:
- Light tan, dark tan, blue for blueberry muffin
- Light brown, brown, dark brown for chocolate muffin
- Brown, white, purple (or any color for mug) for latte

Size F/3.75mm crochet hook

1 pair of 9mm safety eyes for each item

Black embroidery floss

Small embroidery needle

Fiberfill stuffing

Yarn needle

Stitch marker

Scissors

Optional: pink felt and thread for cheeks

Thin cardboard

ABBREVIATIONS

BLO	Back Loops Only
FLO	Front Loops Only
INC	Increase
INV DEC	Invisible Decrease

R	Round or Row
SC	Single Crochet
SL ST	Slip Stitch
ST/S	Stitch/es

FINISHED MEASUREMENTS

MUFFIN

approx. 3 inches wide by 3.5 inches tall

LATTE

approx. 4 inches wide with handle by 2.5 inches tall

MUFFIN

MUFFIN BOTTOM

Using *light tan* **or** *light brown yarn,*

R1   6 sc in magic ring. **(6 sts)**

R2   Inc in each st around. **(12 sts)**

R3   *Sc 1, inc* 6 times. **(18 sts)**

R4   *Inc, sc 2* 6 times. **(24 sts)**

R5   *Sc 3, inc* 6 times. **(30 sts)**

R6   *Inc, sc 4* 6 times. **(36 sts)**

R7   In BLO, *Sc 5, inc* 6 times. **(42 sts)**

R8-13   Sc 42.

Fasten off and leave a long tail for sewing. Add the safety eyes, placing them between rounds 10 and 11, about 4 stitches apart. Sew on the mouth. Add felt cheeks. *(photo 1)*

1

Trace the base of the muffin onto cardboard, cut it out, and place in the bottom of the muffin. *(photo 2)*

2

MUFFiN TOP

Using *dark tan* **or brown yarn,**

R1 6 sc in magic ring. **(6 sts)**

R2 Inc in each st around. **(12 sts)**

R3 *Sc 1, inc* 6 times. **(18 sts)**

R4 *Sc 2, inc* 6 times. **(24 sts)**

R5+6 Sc 24.

R7 *Sc 3, inc* 6 times. **(30 sts)**

R8 *Sc 4, inc* 6 times. **(36 sts)**

R9 *Sc 5, inc* 6 times. **(42 sts)**

R10 Sc 42.

R11 *Sc 6, inc* 6 times. **(48 sts)**

R12 *Sc 6, inv dec* 6 times. **(42 sts)**

R1
3   In FLO, Sc 42.

R1
4   Sc 42.

Fasten off and weave in the ends. *(photo 3)*

3

TO ASSEMBLE THE MUFFIN

With a yarn needle, weave through the back loops leftover from R13 of the muffin top and the stitches of R13 of the muffin bottom *(photos 4+5)* Make sure to weave the needle through the stitches and not over them. This will create a clean finish on the muffin. *(photo 6)* Before closing the piece add fiberfill. Secure and hide the tail. *(photo 7)*

4

5

BLUEBERRiES OR CHOCOLATE CHiPS

MAKE 10

Using *blue* or *dark brown yarn,*

R1   5 sc in magic ring. **(5 sts)**

Sl st into first sc to fasten off. Leave a tail for sewing. *(photo 8)*

With a yarn needle, sew the blueberries or chocolate chips in place around the muffin top. Secure and hide the tails. *(photos 9+10)*

9

10

LATTE

MUG

Using *purple yarn* (or the color of your choice),

R1   6 sc in magic ring. **(6 sts)**

R2   Inc in each st around. **(12 sts)**

R3   *Sc 1, inc* 6 times. **(18 sts)**

R4   *Inc, sc 2* 6 times. **(24 sts)**

R5   In BLO, Sc 24.

R6   *Inc, sc 3* 6 times. **(30 sts)**

R7   *Sc 4, inc* 6 times. **(36 sts)**

R8   Sc 36.

R9   *Sc 5, inc* 6 times. **(42 sts)**

R10   *Inc, sc 6* 6 times. **(48 sts)**

R11-17   Sc 48.

Fasten off and weave in the ends. Add the safety eyes, placing them between rounds 12 and 13, about 4 stitches apart. Sew on the mouth. Add felt cheeks. *(photo 11)*

11

HANDLE

Using *purple yarn* (or the color of your choice),

R1   7 sc in magic ring. **(7 sts)**

R2-19   Sc 7.

Fasten off and leave a tail for sewing. Leave unstuffed. *(photo 12)*

With a yarn needle, sew the handle to the side of the mug. Place the end of the handle (R19) near R5 of the mug and sew in place. *(photo 13)* Fold the top part of the handle over about half an inch and sew near rounds 13–15 of the mug. *(photo 14)* Secure and trim tail.

Using **brown yarn**,

R1   6 sc in magic ring. **(6 sts)**

R2   Inc in each st around. **(12 sts)**

R3   *Sc 1, inc* 6 times. **(18 sts)**

R4   *Inc, sc 2* 6 times. **(24 sts)**

R5   *Sc 3, inc* 6 times. **(30 sts)**

R6   *Inc, sc 4* 6 times. **(36 sts)**

R7   *Sc 5, inc* 6 times. **(42 sts)**

R8   *Inc, sc 6* 6 times. **(48 sts)**

Fasten off and leave a long tail for sewing. *(photo 15)*

15

For the latte art detail, use white yarn and back stitch between the rounds, following the spiral pattern. *(photos 16+17)* Secure and trim the tail.

16

17

TO ASSEMBLE THE COFFEE

Trace the coffee piece and bottom of the mug onto cardboard and cut the pieces out. *(photo 18)* With a yarn needle, weave through the stitches of R8 of the coffee and count down three horizontal rows on the inside of the mug. *(photos 19–22)* Make sure to only go through the horizontal row of stitches from the mug. This will create a clean finish and the stitching will not show on the outside of the mug. About halfway around, add the small cardboard circle to the bottom of the mug, then add fiberfill. *(photo 23)* Add the larger cardboard circle to contain the fiberfill. *(photo 24)* Add any extra fiberfill before closing the piece. Secure and hide the tail. *(photos 25+26)*

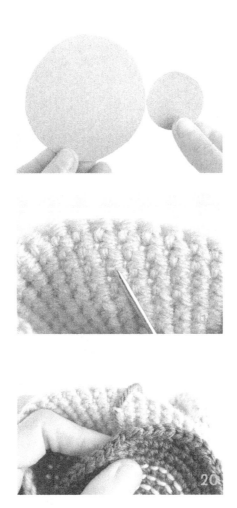

MATERIALS

Worsted weight/4-ply yarn:
- Tan
- Cream
- Brown
- Yellow

Size G/4mm crochet hook

1 pair of 9mm safety eyes

Black embroidery floss

Small embroidery needle

Yarn needle

Stitch marker

Scissors

Optional: pink felt and thread for cheeks

Thick cardboard *(Optional, but this will make the pancakes more round)*

Hot glue gun

ABBREVIATIONS

BLO	Back Loops Only
CH	Chain
INC	Increase

INV DEC	Invisible Decrease
R	Round or Row
SC	Single Crochet
SL ST	Slip Stitch
ST/S	Stitch/es

FINISHED MEASUREMENTS

STACK OF PANCAKES

approx. 4 inches wide

Since the pancake will be flat, the posts of the safety eyes will stick out the back. This can TOTALLY be left as is! But if you'd like them to be flush, use my trick to melt the backs (see Melting the Backs of Safety Eyes, this page). Make sure to fold your work away from the safety eyes and use caution so the work doesn't catch. Adult supervision is required. Do this at your own risk!

PANCAKE

MAKE 3 OR MORE

Using *tan yarn*,

R1   6 sc in magic ring. **(6 sts)**

R2   Inc in each st around. **(12 sts)**

R3   *Sc 1, inc* 6 times. **(18 sts)**

R4   *Inc, sc 2* 6 times. **(24 sts)**

R5   *Sc 3, inc* 6 times. **(30 sts)**

R6   *Inc, sc 4* 6 times. **(36 sts)**

R7   *Sc 5, inc* 6 times. **(42 sts)**

R8   *Inc, sc 6* 6 times. **(48 sts)**

R9   *Sc 7, inc* 6 times. **(54 sts)**

R1
0   *Inc, sc 8* 6 times. **(60 sts)**

Change to *cream yarn*,

R1
1   Sc 60.

Add the safety eyes, placing them between rounds 6 and 7, about 4 stitches apart.

Sew on the mouth. Add felt cheeks. *(photo 1)*

R1
2   In BLO, *Inv dec, sc 8* 6 times. **(54 sts)**

Change to *tan yarn*,

R1
3   *Sc 7, inv dec* 6 times. **(48 sts)**

Trace the pancake on thick cardboard and cut it out. Place the cardboard inside the pancake and crochet the remaining rounds. No fiberfill will be added. *(photo 2)*

R1
4   *Inv dec, sc 6* 6 times. **(42 sts)**

R1
5   *Sc 5, inv dec* 6 times. **(36 sts)**

R1
6   *Inv dec, sc 4* 6 times. **(30 sts)**

R1
7   *Sc 3, inv dec* 6 times. **(24 sts)**

R1
8   *Inv dec, sc 2* 6 times. **(18 sts)**

R1

9   *Sc 1, inv dec* 6 times. **(12 sts)**

R2

0   Inv dec around 6 times. **(6 sts)**

Fasten off and leave a tail for closing the piece. *(photo 3)*

Note: *Not every pancake will need eyes, but you can add them if you'd like!*

Using *brown yarn,*

R1   6 sc in magic ring. **(6 sts)**

R2   Inc in each st around. **(12 sts)**

R3   *Sc 1, inc* 6 times. **(18 sts)**

This next round will form the drips of syrup. After each drip is made, make sure to sl st back into the same space as the sc that was made before beginning the chain.

R4   Sc 2, ch 6 and starting in 2nd ch from hook sc across 5 times. Sl st back into the same space as the sc that was made before beginning the chain. Sc 2, ch 5 and starting in 2nd ch from hook sc across 4 times. Sl st back into the same space as the sc. Sc 3, ch 4 and starting in 2nd ch from hook sc across 3 times. Sl st back into the same space as the sc. Sc 2, ch 5 and starting in 2nd ch from hook sc across 4 times. Sl st back into the same space as the sc. Sc 3, ch 6 and starting in 2nd ch from hook sc across 5 times. Sl st back into the same space as the sc. Sc 2, ch 8 and starting in 2nd ch from hook sc across 7 times. Sl st back into the same space as the sc. Sc 3, ch 7 and starting in 2nd ch from hook sc across 6 times. Sc 1. *(photos 4–7)*

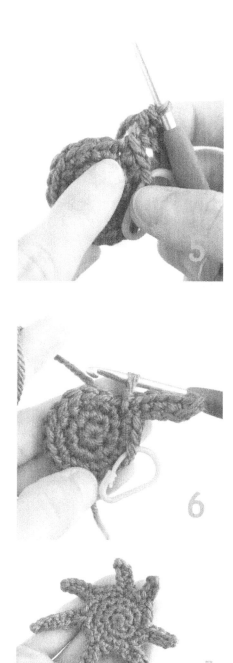

Fasten off and leave a long tail for sewing. With the yarn needle, sew the syrup to the side of the pancake. Make sure to go through the stitches from R4 of the syrup and not over them. *(photo 8)* Use hot glue to attach the drips to the pancake. *(photo 9)* Secure and hide the tail.

Using yellow yarn, Ch 4.

R1   In 2nd ch from hook sc across. **(3 sts)** Ch 1 and turn.

R2+3   Sc 3. Ch 1 and turn after row 2 only. *(photo 10)*

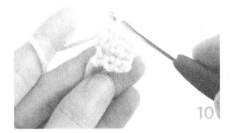

R4   Sc around the three edges. To do this, begin by placing a sc into the same space as the last sc we just made. *(photo 11)* This will help turn the work so we can work along the sides. Sc 1 then inc in the corner space. Sc 1 then inc in the corner space once more. *(photo 12)* Sc 1. Sc into the fourth corner (this acts as an increase in the corner). You will have 12 sts at the end. *(photo 13)*

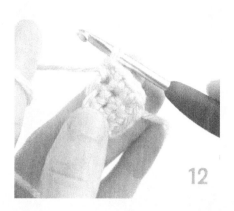

Fasten off and leave a tail for sewing. With the yarn needle, sew the pat of butter on top of the syrup. Secure and hide the tail. *(photo 14)*

MATERIALS

- Worsted weight/4-ply yarn:
  - Light blue
  - Red
  - White
  - Black
  - Yellow
  - Leaf green
  - Bright red
  - Kelly green

- Size F/3.75mm crochet hook

- 8 pairs of 6mm safety eyes

- Black embroidery floss

- Small embroidery needle

- Fiberfill stuffing

- Yarn needle

- Stitch marker

- Scissors

- *Optional:* straight pins to help with assembling pieces

- Thin cardboard

- Hole punch

ABBREVIATIONS

BLO	Back Loops Only
CH	Chain
DC	Double Crochet
FLO	Front Loops Only
HDC	Half Double Crochet
INC	Increase
INV DEV	Invisible Decrease
R	Round or Row
SC	Single Crochet
SL ST	Slip Stitch
ST/S	Stitch/es
TR	Treble Crochet

FINISHED MEASUREMENTS

BOX

approx. 5 inches wide by 3.5 inches deep by 1.5 inches tall

OCTOPUS HOT DOG

approx. 1.5 inches wide by 2.5 inches tall

RICE BALL

approx. 2 inches wide by 2.25 inches tall

EDAMAME

approx. 1 inch wide by 3.5 inches tall

HARD-BOILED EGG

approx. 2 inches wide by 2.5 inches tall

CHERRY TOMATO

approx. 1.5 inches wide by 1.5 inches tall

Using *light blue yarn*, Ch 23.

R1 Starting in the 2nd ch from hook sc across. **(22 sts)** Ch 1 and turn.

R2-17 Sc 22. Ch 1 and turn. Do not ch 1 and turn after row 17.

R18 Sc around the three edges. To do this, begin by placing a sc into the same space as the last sc you just made. *(photo 1)* This will help turn the work so you can work along the sides. Sc 15, then inc in the corner space. *(photos 2+3)* Sc 20 across, then inc in the corner space once more. Sc 15, then sc into the fourth corner—this acts as an increase in the corner. *(photo 4)* Ch 1. You should have 78 sts at the end. Keep in mind that the Ch 1 does not count as a stitch!

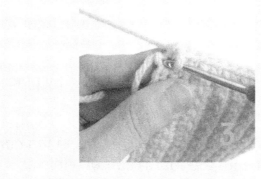

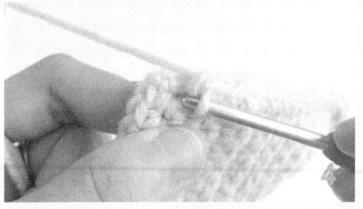

9   In BLO, Sc 78. *(photo 5)*

158

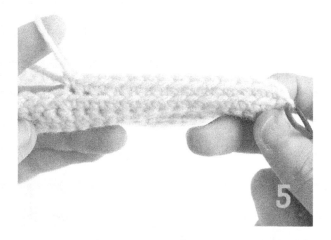

The next rounds will be worked in a continuous spiral. Do not join work.

R20-24 **Sc 78.**

Fasten off and weave in the ends. *(photos 6+7)*

7

OCTOPUS HOT DOG

Using *red yarn*,

R1   6 sc in magic ring. **(6 sts)**

R2   Inc in each st around. **(12 sts)**

R3   *Sc 1, inc* 6 times. **(18 sts)**

R4-10 Sc 18.

Add the safety eyes, placing them between rounds 7 and 8, about 2 stitches apart. Sew on the mouth. *(photo 8)*

8

This next round will make the tentacles.

R1

1   In FLO, *Sc 3, ch 5 and starting in 2nd ch from hook sc across 4 times. Sl st back into the same space as the sc that was made before beginning the chain* 6 times. *(photos 9–11)*

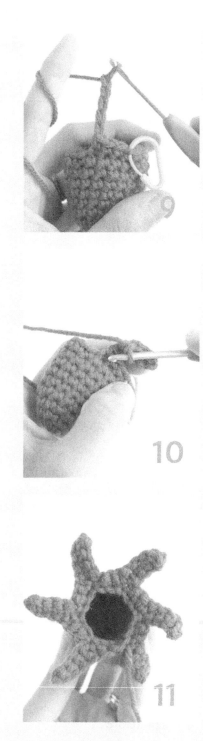

Place a stitch marker in the last back loop, then count 18 sts and that is where **R12** starts. *(photos 12+13)*

R1
2 In BLO leftover from R11, *Sc 1, inv dec* 6 times. **(12 sts)** *(photo 14)*

Begin adding fiberfill and continue as you close the piece.

R1
3 Inv dec around 6 times. **(6 sts)**

Fasten off and leave a tail to close the piece. *(photos 15+16)*

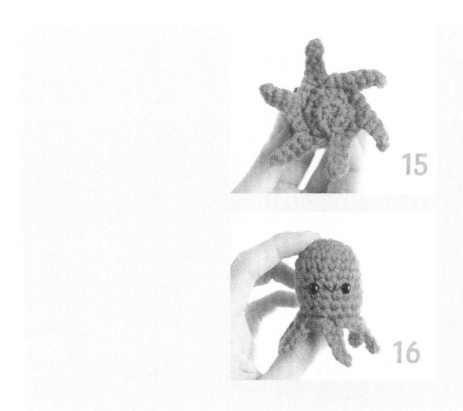

RICE BALL

RICE

Using   ,

R1   6 sc in magic ring. **(6 sts)**

R2   *Sc 1, inc* 3 times. **(9 sts)**

R3   *Sc 2, inc* 3 times. **(12 sts)**

R4   *Sc 3, inc* 3 times. **(15 sts)**

R5   *Sc 4, inc* 3 times. **(18 sts)**

R6   *Sc 5, inc* 3 times. **(21 sts)**

R7   *Sc 6, inc* 3 times. **(24 sts)**

R8   *Sc 7, inc* 3 times. **(27 sts)**

R9+10 Sc 27.

Add the safety eyes, placing them between rounds 7 and 8, about 2 stitches apart. Sew on the mouth. *(photo 17)*

17

R1
1   *Sc 7, inv dec* 3 times. **(24 sts)**

R1
2   *Sc 2, inv dec* 6 times. **(18 sts)**

Begin adding fiberfill and continue as you close the piece.

R1
3   *Sc 1, inv dec* 6 times. **(12 sts)**

R1
4   Inv dec around 6 times. **(6 sts)**

Fasten off and leave a tail for closing the piece. *(photos 18+19)*

18

NORi STRiP

Using **black yarn**, Ch 3.

R1   Starting in the 2nd ch from hook sc across. **(2 sts)** Ch 1 and turn.

R2-13 Sc 2. Ch 1 and turn. *(photo 20)*

20

Do not ch 1 and turn after row 13.

R1

4   Sc around the three edges. To do this, begin by placing a sc into the
       same space as the last sc you just made. This will help turn the work
       so you can work along the sides. Sc 11, then inc in the corner space.

Then inc in the next space. Sc 11. Sc into the fourth corner—this acts as an increase in the corner. You should have 30 sts at the end.

Fasten off and leave a tail for sewing. *(photo 21)*

21

Pin the nori in place on the rice ball. *(photo 22)* With a yarn needle, sew the nori strip in the center of the rice ball. Make sure to go through the stitches from R14 of the nori and not over them. This will give the rice ball a clean finish. *(photo 23)* Secure and hide the tail. *(photo 24)*

22

23

24

EDAMAME

MAKE 3

Using *leaf green*,

R1 5 sc in magic ring. **(5 sts)**

R2 Inc in each st around. **(10 sts)**

R3-5 Sc 10.

R6 Inv dec around 5 times. **(5 sts)** *(photo 25)*

25

R7 Inc in each st around. **(10 sts)** *(photo 26)*

26

R8-10 Sc 10.

Add the safety eyes, placing them between rounds 8 and 9, about 2 stitches apart. Sew on the mouth. *(photo 27)*

27

**R1
1**   Inv dec around 5 times. **(5 sts)**

**R1
2**   Inc in each st around. **(10 sts)**

R13-15 Sc 10.

**R1
6**   Inv dec around 5 times. **(5 sts)**

Fasten off and leave a tail for closing the piece.

Leave unstuffed. *(photos 28+29)*

28

29

HARD-BOILED EGG

Using *yellow yarn*,

R1   6 sc in magic ring. **(6 sts)**

R2   Inc in each st around. **(12 sts)**

R3   *Sc 1, inc* 6 times. **(18 sts)**

Change to   ,

R4   *Sc 2, inc* 6 times. **(24 sts)** *(photo 30)*

30

This next round will build up the top of the egg.

R5   Sc 8, hdc, 2 dc, 2 dc, 2 tr, 2 tr, 2 dc, 2 dc, hdc, sc 8. **(30 sts)** *(photo 31)*

31

R6   In BLO, Sc 30. *(photo 32)*

173

32

Add the safety eyes, placing them between rounds 2 and 3 from the magic ring. Sew on the mouth. *(photo 33)*

33

Trace the flat side of the egg onto a piece of thin cardboard. Cut out the tracing and hole-punch a few holes so the eyes can fit in the holes. Place the cardboard inside the egg. *(photo 34)*

34

R7   *Sc 3, inv dec* 6 times. **(24 sts)** *(photo 35)*

35

R8   Sc 24.

R9   *Sc 2, inv dec* 6 times. **(18 sts)**

Begin adding fiberfill and continue as you close the piece.

R1
0   *Sc 1, inv dec* 6 times. **(12 sts)**

R1
1   Inv dec around 6 times. **(6 sts)**

Fasten off and leave a tail for closing the piece. *(photos 36+37)*

36

37

CHERRY TOMATO

TOMATO

MAKE 2

Using *bright red yarn*,

R1   6 sc in magic ring. **(6 sts)**

R2   Inc in each st around. **(12 sts)**

R3   *Sc 1, inc* 6 times. **(18 sts)**

R4-7 Sc 18.

R8   *Sc 1, inv dec* 6 times. **(12 sts)**

Add the safety eyes, placing them between rounds 6 and 7, about 2 stitches apart. Sew on the mouth. Begin adding fiberfill and continue as you close the piece. *(photo 38)*

39

R9   Inv dec around 6 times. **(6 sts)**

Fasten off and leave a tail for closing the piece.

LEAFY TOP

MAKE 2

Using *kelly green yarn*,

R1   5 sc in magic ring. **(5 sts)**

R2   Inc in each st around. **(10 sts)**

R3   *Sc 2, ch 2 and in 2nd ch from hook sc 1. Sl st back into the same space as the sc that was made before beginning the chain* 5 times. *(photos 39–41)* Fasten off and leave a tail for sewing.

41

With a yarn needle, sew the leafy top to the top of the tomato. *(photo 42)* Make sure to weave the needle through rounds 2 and 3. *(photo 43)* Secure and hide the tail. *(photo 44)*

42

43

Now it's time to build your bento box! Place the items however you'd like, just so long as they all fit inside! *(photos 45+46)*

BURRITO

MATERIALS

X Worsted weight/4-ply yarn:
- Tan
- Green
- Brown
- White
- Yellow
- Gray

X Size G/4mm crochet hook

X 1 pair of 6mm safety eyes

X Black embroidery floss

X Small embroidery needle

X Hot glue gun

X Red felt

X Yarn needle

X Stitch marker

X Scissors

ABBREVIATIONS

CH	Chain
DC	Double Crochet

FLO	Front Loops Only
HOC	Half Double Crochet
INC	Increase
R	Round or Row
SC	Single Crochet
SL ST	Slip Stitch
ST/S	Stitch/es

FINISHED MEASUREMENTS

BURRITO

approx. 2.5 inches wide by 4.5 inches tall

TORTILLA

Using *tan yarn*,

R1   6 sc in magic ring. **(6 sts)**

R2   Inc in each st around. **(12 sts)**

R3   *Sc 1, inc* 6 times. **(18 sts)**

R4   *Inc, sc 2* 6 times. **(24 sts)**

R5   *Sc 3, inc* 6 times. **(30 sts)**

R6   *Inc, sc 4* 6 times. **(36 sts)**

R7   *Sc 5, inc* 6 times. **(42 sts)**

R8   *Inc, sc 6* 6 times. **(48 sts)**

R9   *Sc 7, inc* 6 times. **(54 sts)**

R10   *Inc, sc 8* 6 times. **(60 sts)**

R11   *Sc 9, inc* 6 times. **(66 sts)**

R12   *Inc, sc 10* 6 times. **(72 sts)**

R13   *Sc 11, inc* 6 times. **(78 sts)**

R14   *Inc, sc 12* 6 times. **(84 sts)**

Fasten off and leave a tail for sewing. Add the safety eyes, placing the first eye between rounds 9 and 10 and the second eye between rounds 12 and 13. Make sure to place the eyes on the left side of the tortilla. Sew on the mouth. *(photo 1)* Alternatively, you can add the eyes to the foil instead. (See foil pattern for where to place eyes.)

TO SEW THE BURRITO

Flip the tortilla over so the eyes are now on the right side. *(photo 2)* Starting at the bottom, fold the tortilla up just until the edge meets the magic ring. *(photo 3)* If you look from the other side, there will be about seven rounds from the magic ring to the fold line. *(photo 4)* Fold the left side over halfway. *(photo 5)* Then fold the right side, with the safety eyes, over to the left. *(photo 6)* With the yarn tail, sew the bottom folded pieces of the tortilla together. *(photos 7+8)* Then sew up along the side of the tortilla. *(photo 9)* Only sew up until the two sides meet and form a "v." *(photo 10)* Make sure to weave the needle between the last round of stitches and not over them. This is what the inside will look like. *(photo 11)* Secure and hide the tail. *(photo 12)*

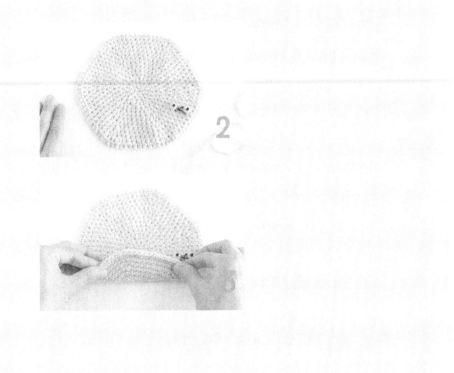

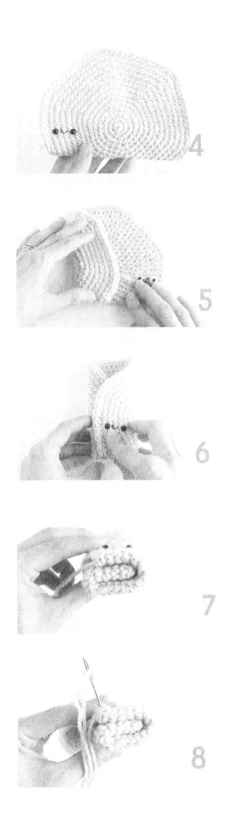

11

12

FOiL

Using *gray yarn*,

R1 6 sc in magic ring. **(6 sts)**

R2 Inc in each st around. **(12 sts)**

R3 *Sc 1, inc* 6 times. **(18 sts)**

R4 *Sc 2, inc* 6 times. **(24 sts)**

R5 *Sc 3, inc* 6 times. **(30 sts)**

R6-16 Sc 30.

R1
7 In FLO, Sc 30. *(photo 13)*

This next round will form the ripples along the foil.

R1
8 *Sc 3, hdc dc hdc, sc 3, hdc dc, dc hdc* 3 times, sc 3. **(42 sts)** *(photo 14)*

14

Fasten off and weave in the ends. If adding the eyes to the foil, place between rounds 10 and 11, about 2 stitches apart. Sew on the mouth.

LETTUCE

Using *green yarn*,

R1   6 sc in magic ring. **(6 sts)**

R2   Inc in each st around. **(12 sts)**

R3   *Sc 1, inc* 6 times. **(18 sts)**

R4   *Inc, sc 2* 6 times. **(24 sts)**

R5   *Sc 3, inc* 6 times. **(30 sts)**

R6   *Inc, sc 4* 6 times. **(36 sts)**

R7   Sc 12, *hdc dc hdc in the next st, sl st in the next st* 7 times, sc 10. **(50 sts)** *(photos 15–17)*

Fasten off and weave in the ends.

MEAT

Using *brown yarn*,

R1   6 sc in magic ring. **(6 sts)**

R2   Inc in each st around. **(12 sts)**

R3   *Sc 1, inc* 6 times. **(18 sts)**

R4   *Inc, sc 2* 6 times. **(24 sts)**

R5   *Sc 3, inc* 6 times. **(30 sts)**

R6   *Inc, sc 4* 6 times. **(36 sts)**

R7   *Sc 5, inc* 6 times. **(42 sts)**

R8   *Inc, sc 6* 6 times. **(48 sts)**

Fasten off and weave in the ends. *(photo 18)*

18

SOUR CREAM

Using   ,

R1   6 sc in magic ring. **(6 sts)**

R2   Inc in each st around. **(12 sts)**

R3   *Sc 1, inc* 6 times. **(18 sts)**

R4   *Inc, sc 2* 6 times. **(24 sts)**

R5   *Sc, sc hdc sc in the next st * 12 times. **(48 sts)** *(photos 19+20)*

Fasten off and weave in the ends.

CHEESE

MAKE 5

Using yellow yarn, Ch 11.

R1   Starting in 2nd ch from hook sl st across. **(10 sts)**

Fasten off and weave in the ends. *(photos 21–24)*

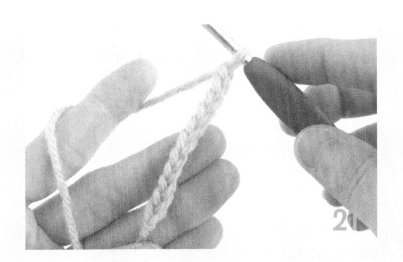

24

TO ASSEMBLE

Lay the lettuce down as the base. *(photo 25)* Fold the meat and sour cream so they're a little wavy and not perfectly folded. *(photos 26+27)* Place on top of the lettuce. *(photo 28)* Place the pieces of cheese in random places between the meat, lettuce, and sour cream. *(photo 29)* Insert the items in the tortilla—they'll fit snug inside! *(photo 30)* Use red felt to cut out small triangles for tomatoes. Use a hot glue gun to attach the tomatoes in various places. *(photo 31)* Then insert the burrito into the foil. *(photos 32+33)*

25

26

27

28

29

30

31

32

33

MATERIALS

Worsted weight/4-ply yarn:
- Tan
- Brown
- Green
- Purple
- White
- Bright red

Size G/4mm crochet hook

1 pair of 9mm safety eyes for pita

2 pairs of 6mm safety eyes for falafel

Black embroidery floss

Small embroidery needle

Fiberfill stuffing

Yarn needle

Stitch marker

Scissors

ABBREVIATIONS

CH	Chain
DC	Double Crochet

HDC	Half Double Crochet
INC	Increase
INV DEC	Invisible Decrease
R	Round or Row
SC	Single Crochet
SK	Skip
SL ST	Slip Stitch
ST/S	Stitch/es

FINISHED MEASUREMENTS

PITA POCKET
approx. 5 inches wide by 3 inches deep by 2 inches tall

FALAFEL
approx. 2 inches wide by 2 inches tall

LETTUCE
approx. 3.5 inches wide

ONION
approx. 2.5 inches wide

TOMATO
approx. 2 inches wide

Using *tan yarn*,

R1   6 sc in magic ring. **(6 sts)**

R2   Inc in each st around. **(12 sts)**

R3   *Sc 1, inc* 6 times. **(18 sts)**

R4   *Inc, sc 2* 6 times. **(24 sts)**

R5   *Sc 3, inc* 6 times. **(30 sts)**

R6   *Inc, sc 4* 6 times. **(36 sts)**

R7   *Sc 5, inc* 6 times. **(42 sts)**

R8   Sc 42.

R9   *Sc 6, inc* 6 times. **(48 sts)**

R10   Sc 48.

R11   *Sc 7, inc* 6 times. **(54 sts)**

R12+13 Sc 54.

R14   *Sc 7, inv dec* 6 times. **(48 sts)**

R15   *Sc 6, inv dec* 6 times. **(42 sts)**

Fasten off and weave in the ends. Add the 9mm safety eyes, placing them between rounds 12 and 13, about 3 stitches apart. Sew on the mouth. *(photo 1)*

1

MAKE 2

Using **brown yarn**,

R1   6 sc in magic ring. **(6 sts)**

R2   Inc in each st around. **(12 sts)**

R3   *Sc 1, inc* 6 times. **(18 sts)**

R4   *Sc 2, inc* 6 times. **(24 sts)**

R5   *Sc 3, inc* 6 times. **(30 sts)**

Add the 6mm safety eyes, placing them between rounds 3 and 4, about 3 stitches apart. Sew on the mouth. *(photo 2)*

2

R6-8 Sc 30.

R9   *Sc 3, inv dec* 6 times. **(24 sts)**

R10   *Sc 2, inv dec* 6 times. **(18 sts)**

Sc 1, inv dec 6 times. **(12 sts)**

Begin adding fiberfill and continue as you close the piece.

Inv dec around 6 times. **(6 sts)**

Fasten off and leave a tail for closing the piece. *(photos 3+4)*

3

4

LETTUCE

MAKE 2

Using *green yarn*,

R1   6 sc in magic ring. **(6 sts)**

R2   Inc in each st around. **(12 sts)**

R3   *Sc 1, inc* 6 times. **(18 sts)**

R4   *Inc, sc 2* 6 times. **(24 sts)**

R5   *Sc 3, inc* 6 times. **(30 sts)**

R6   *Inc, sc 4* 6 times. **(36 sts)**

This next round will form the wavy edge.
Each comma represents a move to the next space.

R7   *Sc, 2 hdc, 2 dc, 2 hdc* 9 times. **(63 sts)** *(photos 5+6)*

5

6

Fasten off and weave in the ends. *(photo 7)*

7

ONION

MAKE 2

Using _____, Ch 18, then sl st into the first ch to form a circle. *(photos 8–10)* Be sure that your chain is not twisted when you start round 1! Ch 1. *(photo 11)* Sl st counts as a stitch, but the ch 1 does NOT count as a stitch.

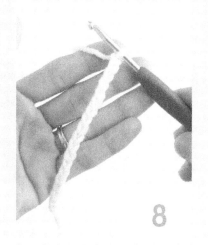

8

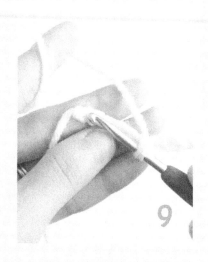

9

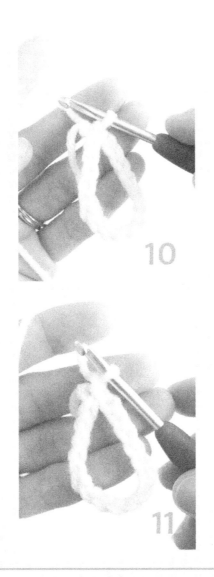

A HELPFUL TIP
Place a stitch marker on the sl st so you know where the last st is.
(photo 12)

R1   *Sc 1, inc* 9 times. **(27 sts)** Make sure to go through both loops.
     (photos 13+14)

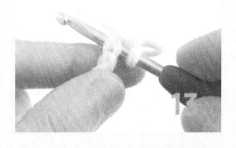

Change to *purple yarn,* *(photo 15)*

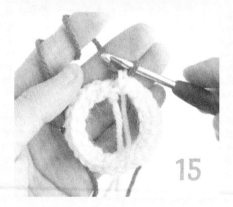

Sc 27.

Fasten off and weave in the ends. *(photo 16)*

16

TOMATO

MAKE 2

Using *bright red yarn*,

R1 6 sc in magic ring. **(6 sts)**

R2 Inc in each st around. **(12 sts)**

R3 Ch 2, dc, *ch 3, sk 1 st, dc, ch 2, dc in the next st* 3 times. *(photos 17-22)* Ch 3, then sl st into the top ch from the start of the round. **(25 sts)**

(photos 23-25) **Note:** *You'll skip the last sc.*

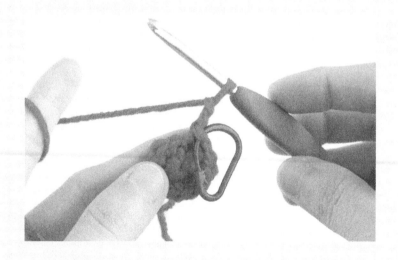

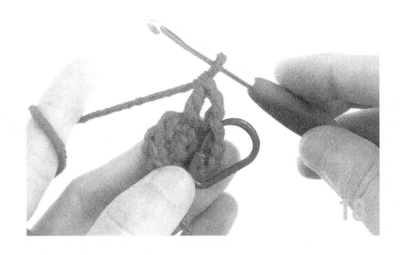

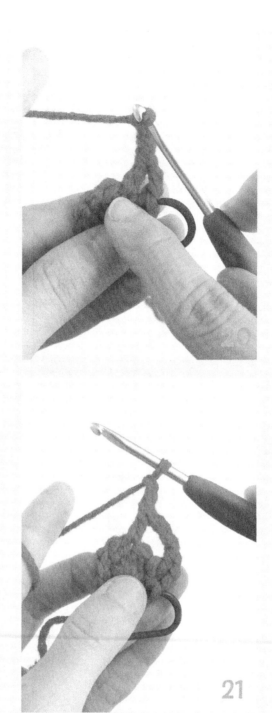

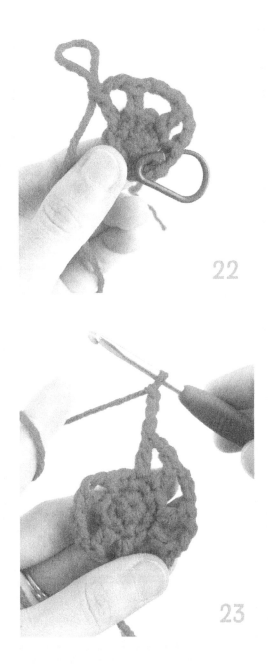

24

25

R4 Sc 25.

Fasten off and weave in the ends. *(photos 26+27)* With the lettuce as the base, place the tomato and onion on top, followed by the falafel. *(photo 28)* Place both stacks side by side in the pita pocket. *(photos 29+30)*

26

27

215

28

29

30

MATERIALS

Worsted weight/4-ply yarn:
- Tan
- Brown
- Orange (for cheese)
- Gray
- Light gray
- Burnt orange
- White

Size F/3.75mm crochet hook

3 pairs of 9mm safety eyes for the sandwiches and bowl

1 pair of 6mm safety eyes for the spoon

Black embroidery floss

Small embroidery needle

Fiberfill stuffing

Yarn needle

Stitch marker

Scissors

Optional: pink felt and thread for cheeks

Thin cardboard

BLO	Back Loops Only
CH	Chain
DC	Double Crochet
HDC	Half Double Crochet
INC	Increase
INV DEC	Invisible Decrease
R	Round or Row
SC	Single Crochet
SL ST	Slip Stitch
ST/S	Stitch/es

FINISHED MEASUREMENTS

FULL GRILLED CHEESE
approx. 4 inches wide by 4 inches tall

HALF GRILLED CHEESE
approx. 3.5 inches wide by 4 inches tall

BOWL OF SOUP
approx. 4.5 inches wide by 2.25 inches tall

SOUP SPOON
approx. 1.5 inches wide at base by 4.5 inches long. Handle is 0.5 inches wide.

BREAD

MAKE 4

Using *tan yarn*, Ch 18.

R1 Starting in 2nd ch from hook sc across. **(17 sts)** Ch 1 and turn.

R2-17 Sc 17. Ch 1 and turn. Do not ch 1 and turn after row 17.

Change to *brown yarn*,

R1

8 Sc around the entire edge. To do this, begin by placing a sc into the same space as the last sc you just made in tan yarn. *(photo 1)* This will help turn the work so you can work along the sides. Sc 15, then inc in the corner space. *(photo 2)* Sc 15, then inc in the corner space. Sc 16, then inc in the corner once more. Sc 16, then sl st into the first st. You will have a total of 69 sts at the end. *(photo 3)*

3

Fasten off. Leave a long tail in brown on just two slices of bread. Weave in all other ends.

CHEESE

Using *orange yarn*, Ch 17.

R1 Starting in 2nd ch from hook sc across. **(16 sts)** Ch 1 and turn.

R2-16 Sc 16. Ch 1 and turn. *(photo 4)*

This next row will form the wavy parts of the cheese around the edges. Make sure to ch 1 and turn after row 16.

7   Sc 3, 2 hdc, 2 dc, 2 hdc, sc 2, 3 hdc, sc 3, hdc dc hdc, sc 2, inc in the corner, 3 hdc, sc 3, hdc dc hdc, sc 3, 3 hdc, sc 3, 2 hdc, sc 1, inc in corner, sc 2, hdc dc hdc, sc 3, 2 hdc, 2 dc, 2 hdc, sc 2, 3 hdc, sc 2, inc in corner, sc 2, 3 hdc, sc 3, hdc dc hdc, sc 3, 3 hdc, sc 4. **(91 sts)** *(photo 5)*

Sl st into the same space as the first sc.
Note: *sl st does not count as a stitch.*

Fasten off and leave a long tail for sewing. *(photo 6)*

TO ASSEMBLE THE GRiLLED CHEESE

1 Add the 9mm safety eyes to the top slice of bread (the slice that has a tail for sewing) and a second slice (one that does not have any tails). Counting from the bottom up, place the eyes between rows 8 and 9, about 3 stitches apart. Sew on the mouth. *(photo 7)*

2 Add the cheese and one more slice of bread (the other slice that does not have any tails) so there are four total pieces touching. *(photo 8)*

3 With the orange tail, sew ONLY the two inside slices of bread that are touching the cheese to the cheese piece. Fold the top slice with the eyes down a bit so you can access the three pieces. *(photo 9)*

4 Weave the needle back and forth through the three pieces. *(photos 10–12)* Make sure to go through the stitches and not over them. A horizontal line of orange stitches will start to form. *(photos 13+14)*

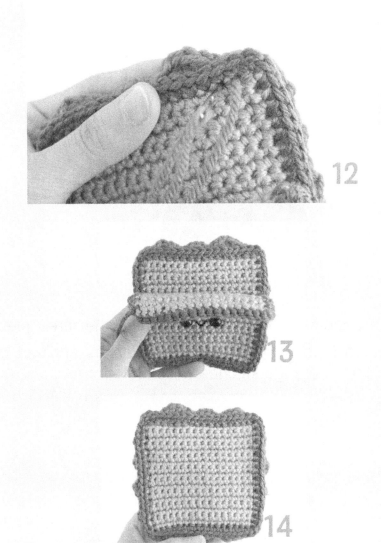

5 Next, sew the top slice of bread to the one it is touching. Make sure to weave the needle through the brown stitches, not over them, to create a clean finish. *(photos 15–17)*

6 Add the last slice of bread to the back. *(photo 18)* This is the other slice that has a brown tail. Repeat the sewing technique in step 5 for this slice. *(photo 19)*

7 Secure with a knot and hide the tails. Add felt cheeks. *(photo 20)*

HALF GRILLED CHEESE

BREAD

MAKE 4

Using *tan yarn*, Ch 2.

R1   In 2nd ch from hook inc. **(2 sts)** Ch 1 and turn.

R2   Inc, sc 1. **(3 sts)** Ch 1 and turn.

R3   Sc 2, inc. **(4 sts)** Ch 1 and turn.

R4   Sc 4. Ch 1 and turn.

R5   Sc 2, inc in the next 2 sts. **(6 sts)** Ch 1 and turn.

R6   Inc, sc 5. **(7 sts)** Ch 1 and turn.

R7   Sc 7. Ch 1 and turn.

R8   Inc in the next 2 sts, sc 5. **(9 sts)** Ch 1 and turn.

R9   Sc 9. Ch 1 and turn.

R10   Inc, sc 8. **(10 sts)** Ch 1 and turn.

R11   Sc 9, inc. **(11 sts)** Ch 1 and turn.

R12   Sc 11. Ch 1 and turn.

R13   Sc 10, inc. **(12 sts)** Ch 1 and turn.

R14   Sc 12. Ch 1 and turn.

R1

5   Sc 11, inc. **(13 sts)** Ch 1 and turn.

R1

6   Inc, sc 12. **(14 sts)** Ch 1 and turn.

R1

7   Sc 13, inc. **(15 sts)** Ch 1 and turn.

R1

8   Sc 15. Ch 1 and turn.

R1

9   Sc 14, inc. **(16 sts)**

Change to *brown yarn,* Ch 1 and turn.

R2

0   Sc 15, inc in last st (the corner space), then sc 18 along the side. **(35 sts)** *(photo 21)*

21

Fasten off. Leave one long tan and one long brown tail on two slices of bread for sewing. Weave in remaining tails.

CHEESE

Using *orange yarn,* Ch 2.

230

R1   In 2nd ch from hook inc. **(2 sts)** Ch 1 and turn.

R2   Inc, sc 1. **(3 sts)** Ch 1 and turn.

R3   Sc 2, inc. **(4 sts)** Ch 1 and turn.

R4   Sc 4. Ch 1 and turn.

R5   Sc 2, inc in the next 2 sts. **(6 sts)** Ch 1 and turn.

R6   Inc, sc 5. **(7 sts)** Ch 1 and turn.

R7   Sc 7. Ch 1 and turn.

R8   Inc in the next 2 sts, sc 5. **(9 sts)** Ch 1 and turn.

R9   Sc 9. Ch 1 and turn.

R10   Inc, sc 8. **(10 sts)** Ch 1 and turn.

R11   Sc 9, inc. **(11 sts)** Ch 1 and turn.

R12   Sc 11. Ch 1 and turn.

R13   Sc 10, inc. **(12 sts)** Ch 1 and turn.

R14   Sc 12. Ch 1 and turn.

R15   Sc 11, inc. **(13 sts)** Ch 1 and turn.

R16   Inc, sc 12. **(14 sts)** Ch 1 and turn.

R17   Sc 13, inc. **(15 sts)** Ch 1 and turn.

R18   Sc 15. Ch 1 and turn.

R19   Sc 14, inc. **(16 sts)** Ch 1 and turn.

This next row will form the wavy parts of the cheese around the two edges.

Sc 3, 3 hdc, sc 3, hdc dc hdc, sc 4, 3 hdc, sc 2, inc in corner, sc 2, 2 hdc, 2 dc, 2 hdc, sc 3, 3 hdc, sc 3, hdc dc hdc, sc 5. **(48 sts)** *(photo 22)*

Fasten off and leave a long tail for sewing.

TO ASSEMBLE THE HALF GRILLED CHEESE

1 Add the 9mm safety eyes to the top slice of bread (the slice that has a tail for sewing) and a second slice (one that does not have any tails). Counting from the bottom up, place the eyes between rows 5 and 6, about 3 stitches apart. Sew on the mouth. *(photo 23)*

2 Add the cheese and one more slice of bread (the other slice that does not have any tails) so there are four total pieces touching. *(photo 24)*

3. With the orange tail, sew ONLY the two inside slices of bread that are touching the cheese to the cheese piece. Fold the top slice with the eyes down a bit so you can access the three pieces. *(photo 25)*

4. Weave the needle back and forth through the three pieces. Make sure to go through the stitches and not over them. A horizontal line of orange stitches will start to form. *(photo 26)*

5. Then turn and sew along the "cut" side of the bread. *(photos 27–29)*

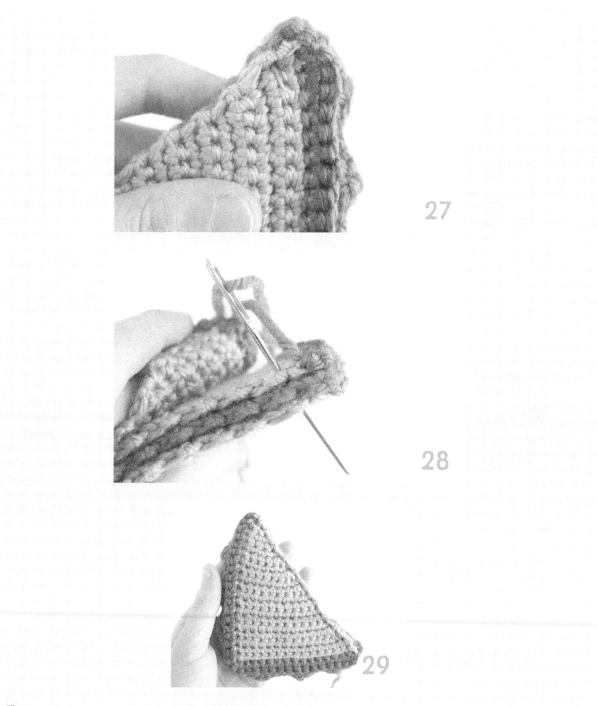

27

28

29

6 Next, sew the top slice of bread to the one it is touching. Make sure to weave the needle through the brown stitches, not over them, to create a clean finish. *(photos 30–32)*

7 Use the tan tail to sew the "cut" side. Make sure to weave the needle over and under the edge. *(photos 33–36)*

34

35

36

8 Add the last slice of bread to the back. This is the slice that has the other brown tail. Repeat the sewing techniques in steps 5 and 6 for this slice. *(photos 37–39)*

37

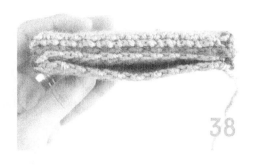

9 Secure and hide the tails. Add felt cheeks. *(photo 40)*

BOWL

Using *light gray yarn*,

R1 6 sc in magic ring. **(6 sts)**

R2 Inc in each st around. **(12 sts)**

R3 *Sc 1, inc* 6 times. **(18 sts)**

R4 *Inc, sc 2* 6 times. **(24 sts)**

R5 *Sc 3, inc* 6 times. **(30 sts)**

R6 *Inc, sc 4* 6 times. **(36 sts)**

R7 *Sc 5, inc* 6 times. **(42 sts)**

R8 In BLO, Sc 42.

R9 *Sc 6, inc* 6 times. **(48 sts)**

R10 *Inc, sc 7* 6 times. **(54 sts)**

R11 Sc 54.

R12 *Inc, sc 8* 6 times. **(60 sts)**

R13 *Sc 9, inc* 6 times. **(66 sts)**

R14-20 Sc 66.

Fasten off and weave in the ends.

Add the 9mm safety eyes, placing them between rounds 15 and 16, about 4 stitches apart. Sew on the mouth. Add felt cheeks. *(photo 41)*

DOLLOP OF

SOUR CREAM

Using _____ , Ch 19.

R1   Starting in 2nd ch from hook sc across. **(18 sts)**

Fasten off and leave a tail for sewing. *(photo 42)*

Starting on the end with no tails, begin rolling the piece up. *(photo 43)* Once you reach the end, use the tail to sew the dollop together. Weave the needle back and forth, making sure all sides are sewn together. *(photo 44)* Set aside.

SOUP

Using *burnt orange yarn*,

R1 6 sc in magic ring. **(6 sts)**

R2 Inc in each st around. **(12 sts)**

R3 *Sc 1, inc* 6 times. **(18 sts)**

R4 *Inc, sc 2* 6 times. **(24 sts)**

R5 *Sc 3, inc* 6 times. **(30 sts)**

R6 *Inc, sc 4* 6 times. **(36 sts)**

R7 *Sc 5, inc* 6 times. **(42 sts)**

R8 *Inc, sc 6* 6 times. **(48 sts)**

R9 *Sc 7, inc* 6 times. **(54 sts)**

R10 *Inc, sc 8* 6 times. **(60 sts)**

1   *Sc 9, inc* 6 times. **(66 sts)**

Fasten off and leave an extra-long tail for sewing. *(photo 45)* With a yarn needle, sew the dollop to the center of the soup. Secure and trim the tail. *(photo 46)*

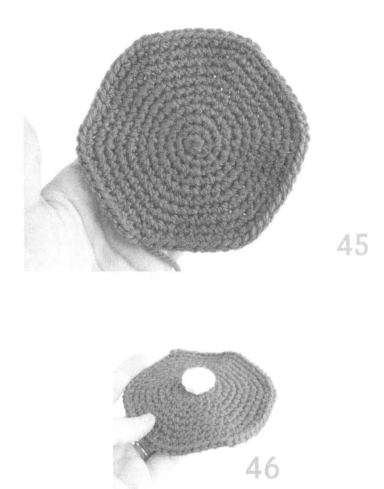

Trace the soup piece onto a piece of thin cardboard. *(photo 47)* On the bowl, count three horizontal lines down. This is where you will attach the soup piece. *(photo 48)* Weave the needle through those horizontal lines and R11 of the soup. *(photos 49–5* Doing this will form a clean line, and the stitching won't show on the outside of the bowl. *(photo 52)* At about the halfway point of attaching the soup, add fiberfill and insert the cardboard piece. *(photo 53)* Continue sewing and add any extra fiberfill before closing completely. Secure and hide the tail. *(photos 54–56)*

47

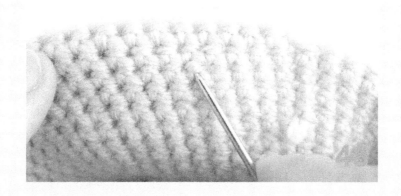

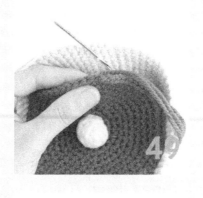

49

50

54

55

SOUP SPOON

Using *gray yarn*,

R1 6 sc in magic ring. **(6 sts)**

R2 Inc in each st around. **(12 sts)**

R3 *Sc 1, inc* 6 times. **(18 sts)**

R4-6 Sc 18.

Add the 6mm safety eyes, placing them between rounds 5 and 6, about 3 stitches apart. Sew on the mouth.

R7 *Sc 1, inv dec* 6 times. **(12 sts)**

R8 *Sc 1, inv dec* 4 times. **(8 sts)**

R9-23 Sc 8.

**R2
4** Inv dec around 4 times. **(4 sts)**

Fasten off and leave a tail for closing the piece. Leave unstuffed. *(photo 57)*

57

MATERIALS

Worsted weight/4-ply yarn:
- Red
- Tan
- Yellow
- Cream
- Yellow
- Bright Red

Size F/3.75mm crochet hook

1 pair of 9mm safety eyes for each condiment bottle

1 pair of 6mm safety eyes for the hot dog

Black and white embroidery floss

Small embroidery needle

Fiberfill stuffing

Yarn needle

Stitch marker

Scissors

Thin cardboard

Optional: hot glue gun, straight pins for assembling the pieces

ABBREVIATIONS

BLO	Back Loops Only
CH	Chain
INC	Increase
INV DEC	Invisible Decrease
R	Round or Row
SC	Single Crochet
ST/S	Stitch/es

FINISHED MEASUREMENTS

HOT DOG
approx. 3.5 inches wide by 4 inches tall

CONDIMENT BOTTLE
approx. 2 inches wide by 4.5 inches tall

HOT DOG

OUTER BUN

MAKE 2

Using *tan yarn,* Ch 15.

In the next row, go through both loops leaving the back "bump." *(photos 1+2)*

R1   Starting in 2nd ch from hook sc across 14 times, turn and sc across 14 times in the back "bumps." **(28 sts)** *(photos 3+4)*

R2 Inc, sc 12, inc in the next 2 sts, sc 12, inc. **(32 sts)**

R3 Inc in the next 2 sts, sc 13, inc in the next 3 sts, sc 13, inc. **(38 sts)**

R4 Inc in the next 3 sts, sc 15, inc in the next 4 sts, sc 15, inc. **(46 sts)**

R5+6 Sc 46.

Fasten off and weave in the ends. *(photos 5+6)*

6

iNNER BUN

MAKE 2

Using cream yarn, Ch 15.

In the next row, go through both loops leaving the back "bump." (See photos 1+2 of the outer bun for reference.)

R1   Starting in 2nd ch from hook sc across 14 times, turn and sc across 14 times in the back "bumps." **(28 sts)** (Again, see photos 3+4 of the outer bun for reference.)

R2   Inc, sc 12, Inc In the next 2 sts, sc 12, Inc. **(32 sts)**

R3   Inc in the next 2 sts, sc 13, inc in the next 3 sts, sc 13, inc. **(38 sts)**

R4   Inc in the next 3 sts, sc 15, inc in the next 4 sts, sc 15, inc. **(46 sts)**

Fasten off and leave a tail for sewing. (photo 7)

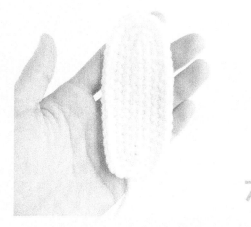

7

TO ASSEMBLE THE BUN

Sew the inner bun to the outer bun. Make sure to weave the needle through the back loops of R6 on the outer bun and R4 of the inner bun. *(photos 8+9)* Make sure to go through the stitches and not over them. *(photos 10+11)* Add fiberfill before closing the pieces, making sure to not overstuff them.

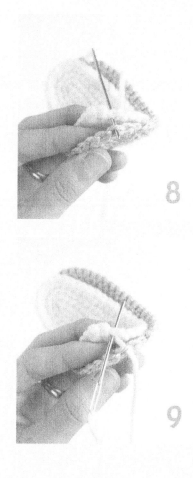

8

9

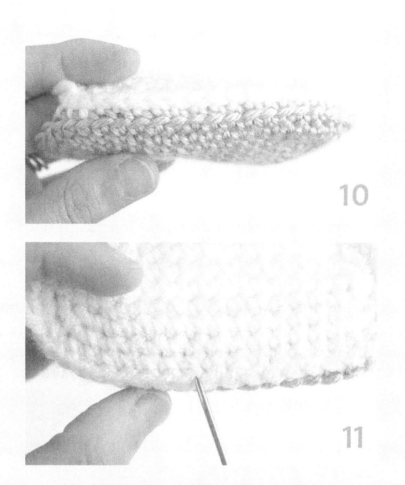

To sew the two bun halves together, place them side by side so the stitches line up. *(photo 12)* With cream yarn, weave the needle through the stitches from R4, sewing about 13 stitches together. *(photos 13–15)* Secure and hide the tail.

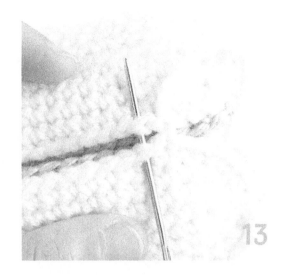

13

14

15

HOT DOG

Using *red yarn*,

R1 5 sc in magic ring. **(5 sts)**

R2 Inc in each st around. **(10 sts)**

R3 *Sc 1, inc* 5 times. **(15 sts)**

R4-19 Sc 15.

Add the 6mm safety eyes, placing them between rounds 14 and 15, about 2 stitches apart. Sew on the mouth. Begin adding fiberfill and continue as you close the piece.

R20 *Sc 1, inv dec* 5 times. **(10 sts)**

R21 Inv dec around 5 times. **(5 sts)**

Fasten off and leave a tail for closing the piece. *(photo 16)*

16

MUSTARD

Using yellow yarn, Ch 32. (photo 17)

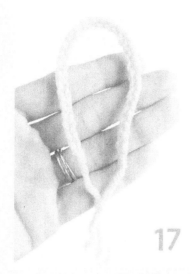

Fasten off and leave a tail for sewing. Sew the mustard to the hot dog. Use pins to place the mustard before sewing. (photo 18)

Optional: Use hot glue to attach the mustard to the hot dog. Secure and hide the tails. (photos 19+20)

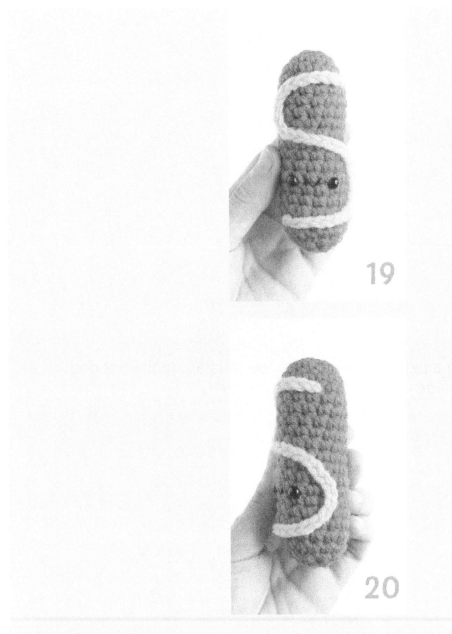

Cut about 12 inches of red yarn and sew the hot dog to the bun. *(photos 21+22)*

21

22

CONDIMENT BOTTLE

LiD

Using *bright red* or *yellow yarn*,

R1   6 sc in magic ring. **(6 sts)**

R2   Inc in each st around. **(12 sts)**

R3   *Sc 1, inc* 6 times. **(18 sts)**

R4   In BLO, Sc 18.

Fasten off and leave a tail for sewing. *(photo 23)* Set aside.

23

Using *bright red* or *yellow yarn*,

R1 4 sc in magic ring. **(4 sts)**

R2 Sc 4.

R3 *Sc 1, inc* 2 times. **(6 sts)**

R4 *Sc 1, inc* 3 times. **(9 sts)**

R5 Sc 9.

Fasten off and leave a tail for sewing. Leave unstuffed. *(photo 24)* With a yarn needle, sew the tip to the center of the lid. *(photo 25)* Secure and trim the tail. Set aside.

24

BOTTLE

Using *bright red* or *yellow yarn*,

R1   6 sc in magic ring. **(6 sts)**

R2   Inc in each st around. **(12 sts)**

R3   *Sc 1, inc* 6 times. **(18 sts)**

R4   *Sc 2, inc* 6 times. **(24 sts)**

R5   *Sc 3, inc* 6 times. **(30 sts)**

R6   In BLO, Sc 30.

R7-21 Sc 30.

Trace the top of the bottle onto a piece of thin cardboard. Cut out and set aside. *(photo 26)* Sew the lid to the top of the bottle. *(photo 27)* Secure and trim the tail. Insert the piece of cardboard. *(photo 28)*

Add the 9mm safety eyes, placing them between rounds 16 and 17, about 3 stitches apart. Sew on the mouth. With white embroidery floss, stitch a "K" or "M" right below the top rim (near rounds 8–12). *(photo 29)*

29

R2
2   In BLO, *Sc 3, inv dec* 6 times. **(24 sts)** Add fiberfill.

Trace the bottom of the bottle onto a piece of thin cardboard. Cut out and place inside the bottom of the bottle. *(photo 30)* Make sure to add enough fiberfill beforehand, as the cardboard will prevent you from adding more.

30

R2
3   *Sc 2, inv dec* 6 times. **(18 sts)**

R2
4   *Sc 1, inv dec* 6 times. **(12 sts)**

R2
5   Inv dec around 6 times. **(6 sts)**

Fasten off and leave a tail for closing the piece. *(photos 31–33)*

31

32

APPLES

MATERIALS

X Worsted weight/4-ply yarn:
- Red or bright green
- Brown
- Forest green
- Light tan

X Size F/3.75mm crochet hook

X 1 pair of 9mm safety eyes for the full apple

X 1 pair of 6mm safety eyes for each apple wedge

X Black embroidery floss

X Small embroidery needle

X Fiberfill stuffing

X Yarn needle

X Stitch marker

X Scissors

X *Optional:* pink felt and thread for cheeks

ABBREVIATIONS

CH	Chain
DC	Double Crochet
DEC	Decrease *(this is not the same as an invisible decrease!)*

HDC	Half Double Crochet
INC	Increase
INV DEC	Invisible Decrease
R	Round or Row
SC	Single Crochet
ST/S	Stitch/es
TR	Treble Crochet

FINISHED MEASUREMENTS

FULL APPLE

approx. 2.75 inches wide by 3.5 inches tall

APPLE WEDGES

approx. 2.5 inches wide by 1.25 inches tall

APPLE

Using *red* or *bright green yarn,*

R1   6 sc in magic ring. **(6 sts)**

R2   Inc in each st around. **(12 sts)**

R3   *Sc 1, inc* 6 times. **(18 sts)**

R4   *Sc 2, inc* 6 times. **(24 sts)**

R5   *Sc 3, inc* 6 times. **(30 sts)**

R6   *Sc 4, inc* 6 times. **(36 sts)**

R7   *Sc 5, inc* 6 times. **(42 sts)**

R8-10 Sc 42.

R11 *Sc 5, inv dec* 6 times. **(36 sts)**

R12   Sc 36.

R13   *Sc 4, inv dec* 6 times. **(30 sts)**

R14-16 Sc 30.

Add the 9mm safety eyes, placing them between rounds 13 and 14, about 3 stitches apart. Sew on the mouth. Add felt cheeks. *(photo 1)*

R17 *Sc 3, inv dec* 6 times. **(24 sts)**

R18+19 Sc 24.

Begin adding fiberfill and continue as you close the piece.

R20 *Sc 2, inv dec* 6 times. **(18 sts)**

R21 *Sc 1, inv dec* 6 times. **(12 sts)**

R22 Inv dec around 6 times. **(6 sts)**

Fasten off and leave a long tail. Close the piece and, before securing the end, make the apple indent at the top and bottom. *(Continued on following page.)*

To do so, insert the needle into the middle of R22 and weave up to the magic ring and pull the tail through. *(photos 2+3)* Tug gently to make the bottom indent and tie a knot. *(photos 4+5)* For the top indent, insert the yarn needle right outside the magic ring. *(photo 6)* Weave the needle through to the bottom of the apple (R22) and pull the tail through. Tug gently to make the top indent. *(photo 7)* Secure and hide the tail. *(photo 8)*

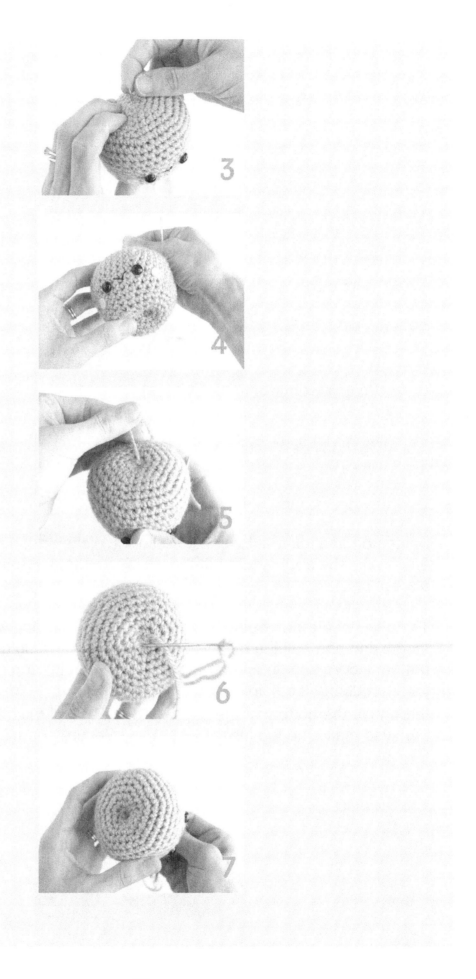

8

STEM

Using **brown yarn,**

R1   5 sc in magic ring. **(5 sts)**

R2-6 Sc 5.

Fasten off and leave a tail for sewing. *(photo 9)* With a yarn needle, sew the stem to the top of the apple where the indent is. *(photo 10)* Secure and hide the tail.

9

LEAF

Using *forest green yarn,* Ch 8. *(photo 11)*

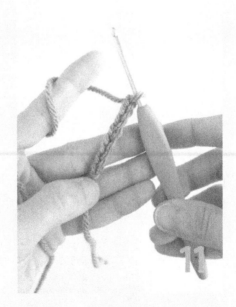

Each comma represents a move to the next ch space.

R1   Starting in 2nd ch from hook sc, hdc, dc, tr, dc, hdc, sc. **(7 sts)**
(photos 12–18)

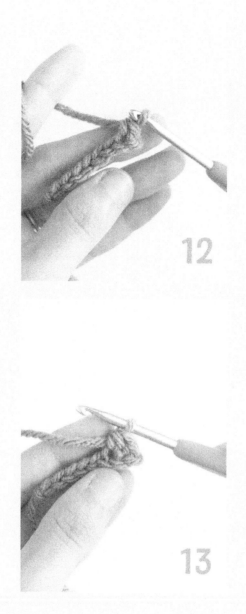

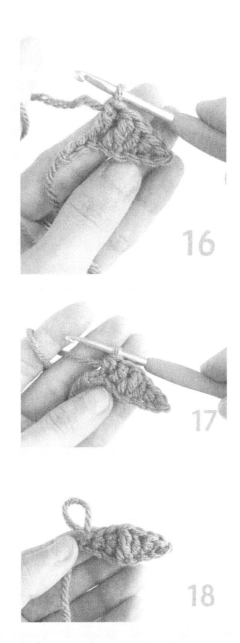

Fasten off and leave a tail for sewing. With the yarn needle, sew the leaf to the top of the apple, right where the stem and apple meet. *(photo 19)* Secure and hide the tail. *(photo 20)*

20

APPLE

Using *light tan yarn,*

R1   6 sc in magic ring. **(6 sts)**

R2   Inc in each st around. **(12 sts)**

R3   *Sc 1, inc* 6 times. **(18 sts)**

R4   *Sc 2, inc* 6 times. **(24 sts)**

R5   *Sc 3, inc* 6 times. **(30 sts)**

Change to *red* or *bright green yarn,*

R6   *Sc 4, inc* 6 times. **(36 sts)** *(photo 21)*

21

Fasten off and weave in the ends. Add the 6mm safety eyes between rounds 3 and 4, about 2 stitches apart. Sew on the mouth. With brown yarn, sew six seeds evenly around the magic ring. *(photo 22)*

22

OUTER SKIN

Using *red* or *bright green yarn,* Ch 2.

R1   In 2nd ch from hook inc. **(2 sts)** Ch 1 and turn.

R2   Inc in each st across. **(4 sts)** Ch 1 and turn.

R3-14 Sc 4. Ch 1 and turn.

R1
5   Dec across 2 times. **(2 sts)** Ch 1 and turn.

R1
6   Dec across 1 time. **(1 st)**

Fasten off and leave a long tail for sewing. *(photo 23)* With a yarn needle, sew the outer skin to the apple wedge. Fold the apple piece in half and line the apple and skin pieces together. *(photo 24)* Start at one end and begin sewing the two pieces together. Make sure to go through the last round of stitches in the apple and not over them. *(photos 25+26)* This will give the apple a clean finish. *(photo 27)* Before closing the piece add fiberfill, making sure to not overstuff. *(photo 28)* Secure and hide the tail. *(photos 29+30)*

23

25

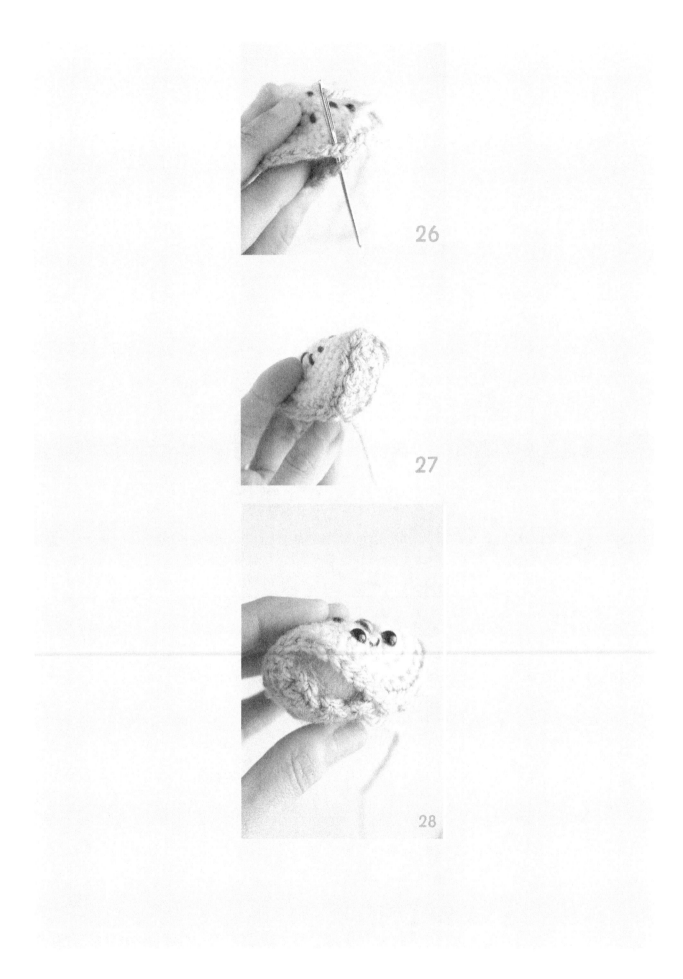

26

27

28

29

30

CHiPS & GUACAMOLE

MATERIALS

✘ Worsted weight/4-ply yarn:
  • Green
  • Gray
  • Tan

✘ Size F/3.75mm crochet hook

✘ 1 pair of 9mm safety eyes for the bowl

✘ 1 pair of 6mm safety eyes for the chip

✘ Black embroidery floss

✘ Small embroidery needle

✘ Fiberfill stuffing

✘ Yarn needle

✘ Stitch marker

✘ Scissors

✘ Straight pins (super helpful when assembling pieces)

ABBREVIATIONS

BO	Bobble
CH	Chain
INC	Increase
R	Round or Row

SC	Single Crochet
SL ST	Slip Stitch
ST/S	Stitch/es

FINISHED MEASUREMENTS

CHIP

approx. 3 inches wide by 2 inches tall

BOWL

approx. 3 inches wide by 3.25 inches tall

Since the chip will be flat, the posts of the safety eyes will stick out the back. This can TOTALLY be left as is! But if you'd like them to be flush, use my trick to melt the backs (see Melting the Backs of Safety Eyes, this page). Make sure to fold your work away from the safety eyes and use caution so the work doesn't catch. Adult supervision is required. Do this at your own risk!

CHIP

Using *tan yarn,*

R1   6 sc in magic ring. **(6 sts)**

R2   Sc 6.

R3   Inc in each st around. **(12 sts)**

R4   *Sc 1, inc* 6 times. **(18 sts)**

R5   Sc 18.

R6   *Sc 2, inc* 6 times. **(24 sts)**

R7-9 Sc 24.

Fasten off and leave a tail for sewing. Add the 6mm safety eyes, placing them between rounds 7 and 8, about 2 stitches apart. Sew on the mouth. *(photo 1)*

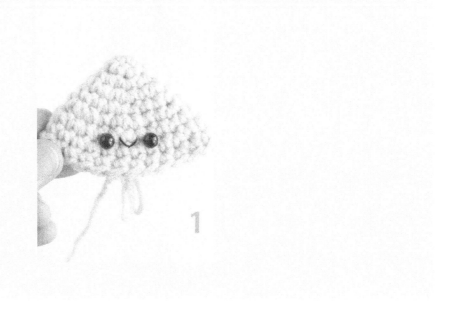

Fold the chip in half so it's flat, and line up the stitches. *(photo 2)* Weave the needle up through the stitches from R9 and not over them. *(photos 3–5)* This will give the edge a clean finish. Leave the chip unstuffed. *(photos 6+7)*

7

GUACAMOLE

FOR CHiP

Using *green yarn*,

R1   6 sc in magic ring. **(6 sts)**

R2   Sc 6.

R3   Inc in each st around. **(12 sts)**

R4   *Sc 1, inc* 6 times. **(18 sts)**

This next round will form the dripping parts of the guac. After each drip is made, make sure to sl st back into the same space as the sc that was made before beginning the chain.

R5   Sc 2, ch 3 and starting in 2nd ch from hook sc across 2 times. Sl st back into the same space as the sc that was made before beginning the chain. Sc 4, ch 5 and starting in the 2nd ch from hook sc across 4 times. Sl st back into the same space as the sc. Sc 4, ch 3 and starting in the 2nd ch from hook sc across 2 times. Sl st back into the same space as the sc. Sc 4, ch 4 and starting in the 2nd ch from hook sc across 3 times. Sl st back into the same space as the sc. Sc 4. *(photos 8–11)*

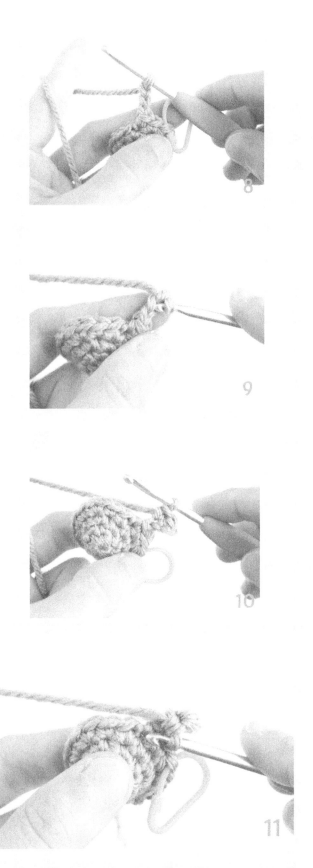

Fasten off and leave a tail for sewing. With the yarn needle, sew the guacamole onto the chip. Make sure to go through the stitches in R5 of the guacamole and not over them. This will give the guacamole a clean finish. *(photo 12)* Secure and hide the tail.

BOWL

Using *gray yarn,*

R1   6 sc in magic ring. **(6 sts)**

R2   Inc in each st around. **(12 sts)**

R3   *Sc 1, inc* 6 times. **(18 sts)**

R4   *Sc 2, inc* 6 times. **(24 sts)**

R5   *Sc 3, inc* 6 times. **(30 sts)**

R6   *Sc 4, inc* 6 times. **(36 sts)**

R7   *Sc 5, inc* 6 times. **(42 sts)**

R8-13 Sc 42.

Fasten off and leave a very long tail for sewing. Add the 9mm safety eyes, placing them between rounds 10 and 11, about 4 stitches apart. Sew on the mouth. *(photo 13)*

13

GUACAMOLE

FOR BOWL

Using *green yarn,*

R1   6 sc in magic ring. **(6 sts)**

R2   Inc in each st around. **(12 sts)**

R3   *Sc 1, inc* 6 times. **(18 sts)**

The next few rounds will build the "lumps" in the guacamole.

R4   *Sc 2, inc, BO, sc 1, inc* 3 times. **(24 sts)** *(photo 14)*

14

R5   *BO, sc 2, inc, sc 3, inc* 3 times. **(30 sts)** *(photo 15)*

15

R6   *Sc 4, inc* 6 times. **(36 sts)** *(photo 16)*

16

R7   *Sc 4, BO, inc, sc 3, BO, sc 1, inc* 3 times. **(42 sts)** *(photo 17)*

17

R8+9 Sc 42. *(photo 18)*

18

Fasten off and weave in the end.

TO SEW THE GUACAMOLE TO THE BOWL

Using the gray yarn tail from the bowl, sew the guacamole to the bowl. Bring the yarn needle from the back of the guacamole piece, between R8+9, to the front and insert needle between R12+13 of the bowl. *(photos 19+20)* Move over to the next stitch and insert the needle. *(photo 21)* Then weave the needle back into the same stitch shown in photo 19. *(photo 22)* Move the needle to the next stitch on the guacamole, coming from the back to the front again. *(photo 23)* Insert the needle into the same space on the bowl. *(photo 24)* Repeat this technique all the way around. You'll see a pattern with the sewing start to form. The stitches will look like "Vs." *(photo 25)* On the back side of the guacamole a horizontal row of gray stitches will form. *(photo 26)* Add fiberfill before closing the piece. Secure and hide the tail. *(photos 27+28)*

19

Using *gray yarn,*

R1   6 sc in magic ring. **(6 sts)**

R2   Sc 6.

R3   *Sc 1, inc* 3 times. **(9 sts)**

R4   Sc 9.

R5   *Sc 2, inc* 3 times. **(12 sts)**

Fasten off and leave a tail for sewing. Add fiberfill. *(photo 29)*

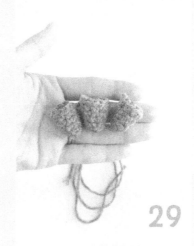

With straight pins, pin the legs in place. Put two legs in the front and one in the back. *(photo 30)* Sew each leg about 2 rounds away from the magic ring. Secure and hide the tails. *(photo 31)*

31

MATERIALS

✖ Worsted weight/4-ply yarn:
  • Purple, pink, or blue
  • White
  • Light gray

✖ Size F/3.75mm crochet hook

✖ 1 pair of 9mm safety eyes

✖ Black embroidery floss

✖ Small embroidery needle

✖ Fiberfill stuffing

✖ Pipe cleaner, measuring 3.5 inches

✖ Yarn needle

✖ Stitch marker

✖ Scissors

✖ *Optional:* pink felt and thread for cheeks and colored felt for adding fruit details

✖ Hot glue gun

ABBREVIATIONS

BLO	Back Loops Only
CH	Chain

INC	Increase
R	Round or Row
SC	Single Crochet
SL ST	Slip Stitch
ST/S	Stitch/es

FINISHED MEASUREMENTS

JUICE BOX

approx. 1.5 inches wide by 5.5 inches tall

JUICE BOX

Note: *This pattern is worked from the top down.*
Make sure to place your eyes accordingly and use photo 8 as a reference.

Using the colored yarn of your choice, Ch 12.

R1 Starting in 2nd ch from hook sc across. **(11 sts)** Ch 1 and turn.

R2-5 Sc 11. Ch 1 and turn. *(photo 1)* Do not ch 1 and turn after row 5.

R6 Sc around the three edges. To do this, begin by placing a sc into the same space as the last sc you just made. *(photo 2)* This will help turn the work so you can work along the sides. Sc 3, then inc in the corner space. *(photo 3)* Sc 9 across, then inc in the corner space once more. *(photo 4)* Sc 3. Sl st into the last st. *(photo 5)* Ch 1. You should have 32 sts at the end. Keep in mind that Ch 1 does not count as a stitch!

R7 In BLO, sc 32. *(photo 6)*

The next rounds will be worked in a continuous spiral. Do not join work.

R8-11 Sc 32.

Change to

R12-18 Sc 32. *(photo 7)*

Add the safety eyes, placing them between rounds 15 and 16, about 3 stitches apart. Sew on the mouth. Add felt cheeks and felt fruit details (see note on this page). *(photo 8)*

9   Sc 2 in white, change to colored yarn, and sc 30. **(32 sts)** *(photos 9+10)*

R20-22 Sc 32.

R23 Sc 32, then sc 4. The extra stitches help even out the piece. *(photo 11)* Make sure to move the stitch marker to the end of the fourth sc.

R24 In BLO, sc 12. Ch 1 and turn. (This will form the bottom flap of the box.) *(photo 12)*

We will now be working the piece flat.

R25-29 Sc 12. Ch 1 and turn. *(photo 13)* Do not ch 1 and turn after row 29.

Fasten off and leave a tail for sewing. Add fiberfill. *(photo 14)*

14

TO SEW THE FLAP TO THE BOX

Count 4 stitches up the side, then count 12 stitches across, placing stitch markers on the first and twelfth stitches. *(photo 15)* This will make sure the 12 stitches on the flap line up properly with the stitches on the box. Weave the needle through the stitches from R29 and the back loops from R23. *(photos 16+17)* Weaving through, not over, the stitches creates a clean seam on the juice box. *(photo 18)* Sew up the short sides, adding any extra fiberfill to the box before closing. Secure and hide the tail. *(photos 19+20)*

15

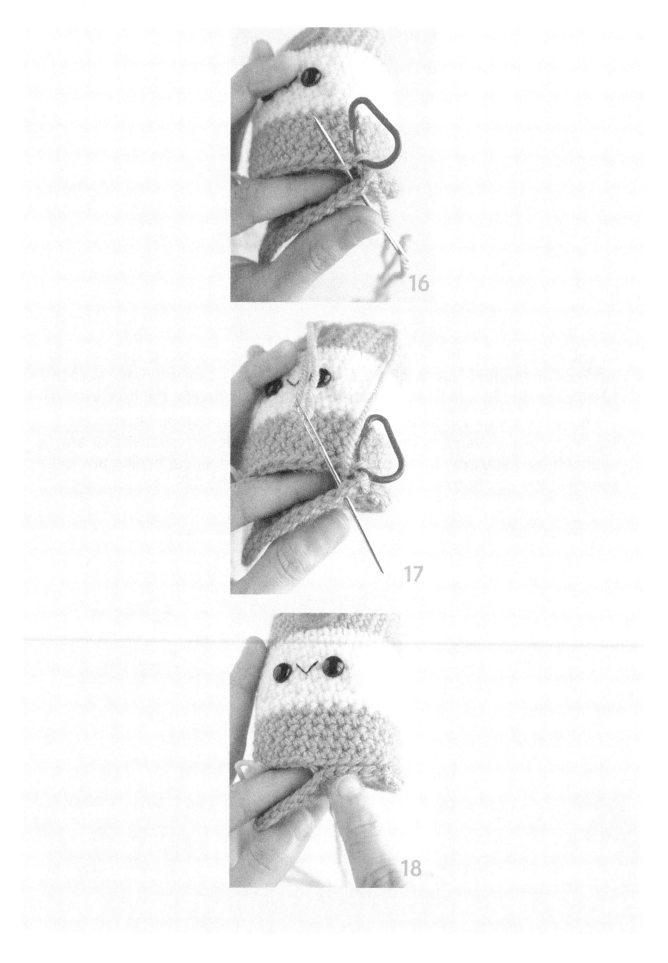

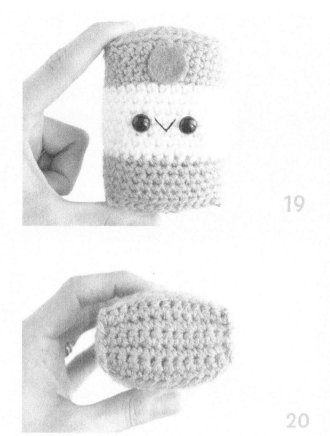

19

20

> **NOTE:** For adding felt fruit details, cut small shapes for a blueberry, apple, strawberry, or grapes. Use hot glue to attach the fruit detail to the juice box. Place in the section of color just above the white middle part.

STRAW

Using *light gray yarn*,

R1   6 sc in magic ring. **(6 sts)**

R2-12 Sc 6.

Fasten off and leave a tail for sewing.

Insert the pipe cleaner into the straw piece. *(photo 21)* A little will stick out the end, and that's okay! Insert the remaining pipe cleaner into the top of the juice box, on the right side near rows 3 and 4. *(photo 22)* With the yarn needle, sew the straw to the juice box. Secure and hide the tail. Bend the straw about half an inch at the top. *(photo 23)*

21

22

23

NOTE: For safety, if giving this to small children, fold the tip of the pipe cleaner about half an inch before inserting it into the straw piece. This way the pipe cleaner doesn't accidentally poke out the top of the straw while being played with.

MATERIALS

- Worsted weight/4-ply yarn:
  - Bright orange
  - Lime green
  - White
  - Orange

- Size F/3.75mm crochet hook

- 2 pairs of 9mm safety eyes

- Black and white embroidery floss

- Small embroidery needle

- Fiberfill stuffing

- Yarn needle

- Stitch marker

- Scissors

- *Optional:* pink felt and thread for cheeks

ABBREVIATIONS

BLO	Back Loops Only
CH	Chain
DC	Double Crochet
HDC	Half Double Crochet
INC	Increase

INV DEC	Invisible Decrease
R	Round or Row
SC	Single Crochet
ST/S	Stitch/es
TR	Treble Crochet

FINISHED MEASUREMENTS

FULL ORANGE

approx. 2.5 inches wide by 2.5 inches tall

HALF ORANGE

approx. 1.5 inches wide by 2.5 inches tall

FULL ORANGE

Using *lime green yarn*,

R1   6 sc in magic ring. **(6 sts)**

Change to *bright orange yarn*, *(photo 1)*

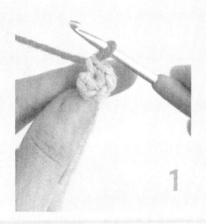

R2   Inc in each st around. **(12 sts)** *(photo 2)*

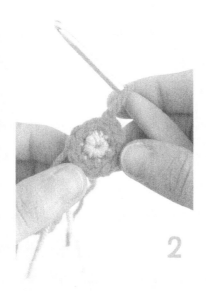

2

R3 *Sc 1, inc* 6 times. **(18 sts)**

R4 *Sc 2, inc* 6 times. **(24 sts)**

R5 *Sc 3, inc* 6 times. **(30 sts)**

R6 *Sc 4, inc* 6 times. **(36 sts)**

R7-13 Sc 36.

Add the safety eyes, placing them between rounds 11 and 12, about 4 stitches apart. Using black embroidery floss, sew on mouth. Add felt cheeks. *(photo 3)*

3

R1
4 *Sc 4, inv dec* 6 times. **(30 sts)**

R1
5 *Sc 3, inv dec* 6 times. **(24 sts)**

R1

6   *Sc 2, inv dec* 6 times. **(18 sts)**

Begin adding fiberfill and continue as you close the piece.

R1

7   *Sc 1, inv dec* 6 times. **(12 sts)**

R1

8   Inv dec around 6 times. **(6 sts)**

Fasten off and leave a tail for closing the piece. *(photo 4)*

4

LEAF

Using *lime green yarn*, Ch 8. *(photo 5)*

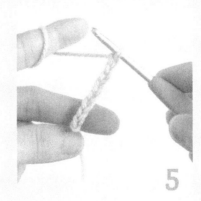

5

Each comma represents a move to the next ch space.

R1 Starting in 2nd ch from hook sc, hdc, dc, tr, dc, hdc, sc. **(7 sts)**
(photos 6–12)

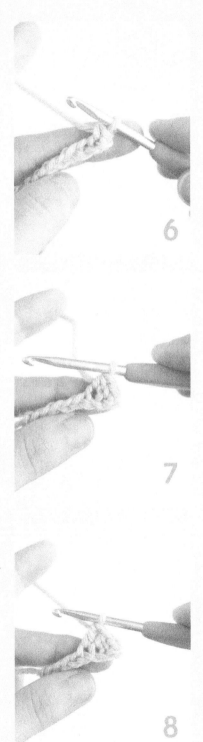

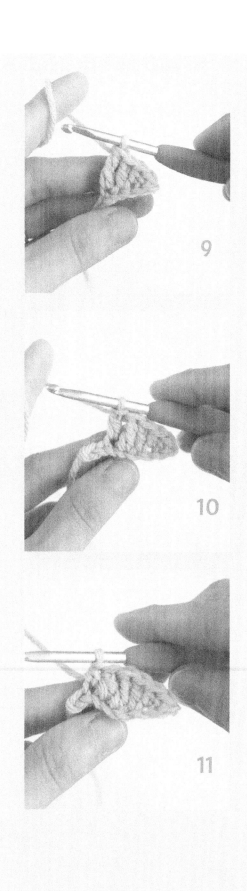

12

Fasten off and leave a tail for sewing. With the yarn needle, sew the leaf to the top of the orange near the green stem. *(photo 13)* Secure and hide the tail. *(photo 14)*

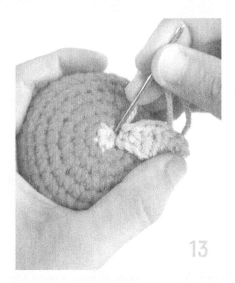

13

14

HALF ORANGE

Using   ,

R1   6 sc in magic ring. **(6 sts)**

Change to *orange yarn*, *(photo 15)*

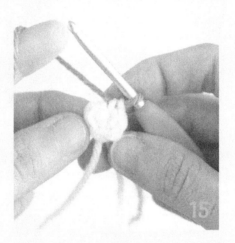

R2   Inc in each st around. **(12 sts)** *(photo 16)*

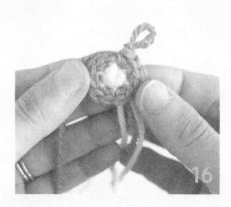

R3   *Sc 1, inc* 6 times. **(18 sts)**

R4 *Inc, sc 2* 6 times. **(24 sts)**

R5 *Sc 3, inc* 6 times. **(30 sts)**

R6 *Inc, sc 4* 6 times. **(36 sts)**

Add the safety eyes, placing them between rounds 3 and 4 on the sides of the magic ring. Using black embroidery floss, sew on mouth. *(photo 17)* If making a winking eye, only attach one safety eye and sew the other with black embroidery floss.

17

Change to *bright orange yarn,*

R7 In BLO, Sc 36. *(photo 18)*

18

Cut a long piece of white embroidery floss and, starting at the magic ring, make six long lines around the face. *(photo 19)* Make sure to space them evenly and go to the rim of the orange. Then backstitch around the entire edge of the orange. *(photo 20)* Secure with a knot and trim the end.

19

20

R8-10 Sc 36.

R1

1   *Sc 4, inv dec* 6 times. **(30 sts)**

R1

2   *Sc 3, inv dec* 6 times. **(24 sts)**

R1

3   *Sc 2, inv dec* 6 times. **(18 sts)**

Begin adding fiberfill and continue as you close the piece.

R1

4   *Sc 1, inv dec* 6 times. **(12 sts)**

R1

5   Inv dec around 6 times. **(6 sts)**

Fasten off and leave a tail for closing piece. *(photo 21)*

21

MATERIALS

✖ Worsted weight/4-ply yarn:
- Red
- White
- Cream

✖ Size G/4mm crochet hook

✖ 1 pair of 9mm safety eyes for the container

✖ 1 pair of 6mm safety eyes for each popcorn kernel

✖ Black embroidery floss

✖ Small embroidery needle

✖ Fiberfill stuffing

✖ Yarn needle

✖ Stitch marker

✖ Scissors

✖ *Optional:* pink felt and thread for cheeks and white felt and thread for label

✖ Thin cardboard

ABBREVIATIONS

BLO	Back Loops Only
CH	Chain
FLO	Front Loops Only

HDC	Half Double Crochet
INC	Increase
INV DEC	Invisible Decrease
R	Round or Row
SL ST	Slip Stitch
ST/S	Stitch/es
SC	Single Crochet

FINISHED MEASUREMENTS

POPCORN CONTAINER

approx. 4.75 inches wide by 2.5 inches deep by 4.5 inches tall

POPCORN

approx. 1.5 inches wide by 1.25 inches tall

CONTAINER

BASE

Using _____, Ch 15.

R1 Starting in 2nd ch from hook sc across. **(14 sts)** Ch 1 and turn.

R2-10 Sc 14. Ch 1 and turn. Do not ch 1 and turn after row 10.

R11

1   Sc around the three edges. To do this, begin by placing a sc into the same space as the last sc you just made. *(photo 1)* This will help turn the work so you can work along the sides. Sc 8, then inc in the corner space. *(photos 2+3)* Sc 12 across, then inc in the corner space once more. Sc 8. Then sc into the fourth corner. *(photo 4)* You will have 48 sts at the end. Fasten off and leave a long tail for sewing. *(photo 5)*

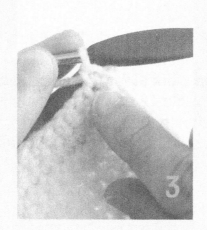

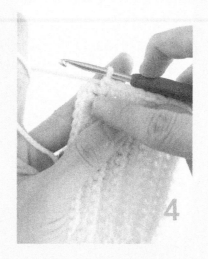

NOTE

There are several color changes for this piece. When changing colors, simply drop the old color, pick up the new color, and continue crocheting as normal. There are only four times when you'll need to carry the red yarn, and those instances are noted throughout the pattern. There are also 4 times where you will need to cut the white yarn and those are noted throughout the pattern. This pattern is written so that when there is a color change, all you have to do is carry the yarn up the few rows where it was last dropped.

BACK PANEL

Using *red yarn*, Ch 21.

R1   Starting in 2nd ch from hook sc across. **(20 sts)** Ch 1 and turn.

R2+3   Sc 20. (Ch 1 and turn after row 2 only.) Change to *white yarn,* Ch 1 and turn. *(photo 6)*

R4-6 Sc 20. (Ch 1 and turn after rows 4 and 5 only.) On row 6, carry red yarn in FRONT of the work. *(photos 7+8)*

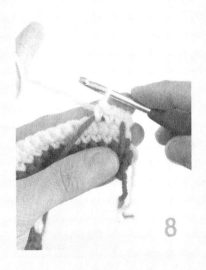

Change to *red yarn*, Ch 1 and turn. *Note: When changing to red yarn, bring white yarn forward.* Yarn over with red and continue with the ch 1 and turn. *(photos 9–11)* Drop the white yarn and leave for R9-11.

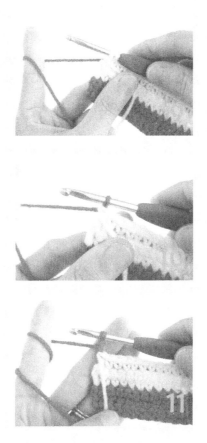

R7+8 Sc 20. (Ch 1 and turn after row 7 only.) Change to *white yarn,* Ch 1 and turn.

Note: *When changing to white yarn, bring red yarn forward.* Yarn over with white and continue with ch 1 and turn. *(photo 12)* Drop the red yarn and leave for R12-14.

R9-11 Sc 20. (Ch 1 and turn after rows 9 and 10 only.) On row 11, carry red yarn in BACK of the work. *(photo 13)*

Change to *red yarn*, Ch 1 and turn. At this point, cut the white yarn and leave a tail long enough to weave in.

R12-14 Sc 20. Ch 1 and turn.

The finished back panel will look like *photo 14* after row 14.

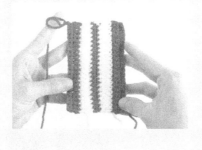

SiDE PANEL

R1
5   In BLO, Sc 20. Ch 1 and turn. *(photo 15)*

R1
6   Sc 20.

Change to   , Ch 1 and turn. *Note: When changing to white yarn, bring red yarn forward.* Yarn over with white and continue with the ch 1 and turn. *(photo 16)*

R17+18 Sc 20. (Ch 1 and turn after row 17 only.) Change to *red yarn,* Ch 1 and turn.

R19+20 Sc 20. (Ch 1 and turn after row 19 only.) Change to   , Ch 1 and turn.

R21+22 Sc 20. (Ch 1 and turn after row 21 only.) Change to *red yarn*, Ch 1 and turn. At this point, cut the white yarn and leave a tail long enough to weave in.

R23+24 Sc 20. Ch 1 and turn.

The finished side panel will look like photo 17 after row 24. *(photo 17)* On the right side you'll see where we picked up the yarn. *(photo 18)* This will be covered when we crochet the top border at the end.

Continue with the front and last side panel. Follow photos 6 through 17 for the color-changing tips provided for the other side panel.

FRONT PANEL

R2
5   In BLO, Sc 20. Ch 1 and turn.

R26+27 Sc 20. (Ch 1 and turn after row 26 only.)
Change to   , Ch 1 and turn.

R28-30 Sc 20. (Ch 1 and turn after rows 28 and 29 only.) On row 30, carry red yarn in FRONT of the work.
Change to *red yarn*, Ch 1 and turn.

R31+32 Sc 20. (Ch 1 and turn after row 31 only.) Change to   ,
Ch 1 and turn.

R33-35 Sc 20. (Ch 1 and turn after rows 33 and 34 only.) On row 35, carry red yarn in BACK of the work. At this point, cut the white yarn and leave a tail long enough to weave in.
Change to *red yarn*, Ch 1 and turn.

R36-38 Sc 20. Ch 1 and turn.

FINAL SIDE PANEL

R3
9   In BLO, Sc 20. Ch 1 and turn.

R4
0   Sc 20.
Change to   , Ch 1 and turn.

R41+42 Sc 20. (Ch 1 and turn after row 41 only.)
Change to *red yarn*, Ch 1 and turn.

R43+44 Sc 20. (Ch 1 and turn after row 43 only.)
Change to   , Ch 1 and turn.

R45+46 Sc 20. (Ch 1 and turn after row 45 only.)
Change to *red yarn*, Ch 1 and turn. At this point, cut the white yarn and leave a tail long enough to weave in.

R47+48 Sc 20. (Ch 1 and turn after row 47 only.)

Fasten off and leave a long red tail for sewing up the side. There will be 8 white tails to weave in. *(photo 19)* Add the 9mm safety eyes, placing the first eye between rows 29 and 30, and the second eye between rows 34 and 35. Count from the bottom up about 8 or 9 rows. Sew on the mouth. Add felt cheeks. *(photo 20)*

19

To make the top border, join red yarn in the upper right-hand corner of the piece. Ch 1. *(photos 21+22)* Sc across the side, note the ch 1 will count as a st. **(48 sts)** *(photos 23+24)* Fasten off and weave in the end.

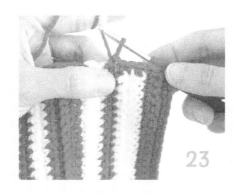

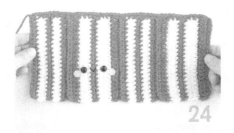

TO ASSEMBLE THE CONTAINER

Start by lining up the edges. *(photo 25)* Next find the back loop from R1—it's a horizontal line. *(photo 26)* Now find the back loop from R48. *(photo 27)* Weave the yarn needle up through the horizontal line in R1 *(photo 28)*, then come down and bring the needle through the middle of the stitch in R48. *(photo 29)* Repeat this technique until you reach the end. The seam will look like *photos 30+31*. Secure and weave in the ends. *(photos 32+33)*

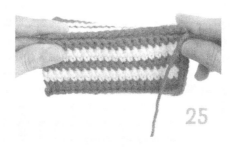

339

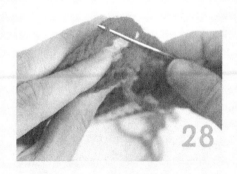

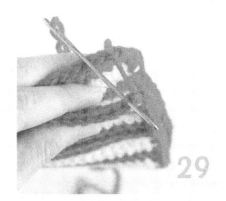

29

30

31

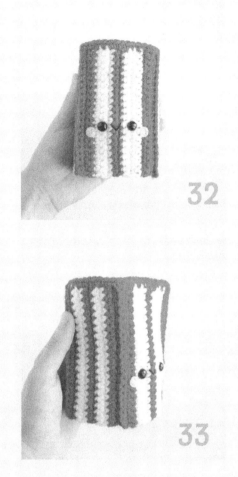

32

33

For the white base, line up the stitches on the base with the bottom of the container. *(photo 34)* With the yarn needle, weave up through the side of the container, then weave the needle from back to front on the white base. *(photos 35+36)* Move to the next stitch and continue weaving the needle back and forth. *(photos 37+38)*

34

35

36

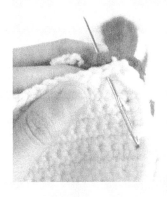

37

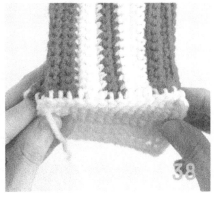

38

Finally, cut a piece of cardboard that is slightly smaller than the base. Place the cardboard in the bottom of the container. *(photo 39)*

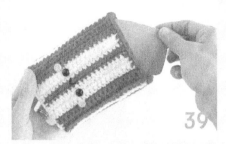

On white felt, stitch the word "Popcorn" using black embroidery floss. Use white embroidery floss to sew the felt to the middle of the container. *(photo 40)*

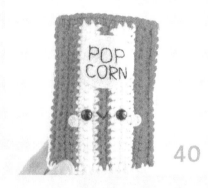

POPCORN

MAKE AS MANY AS YOU NEED TO FILL YOUR CONTAINER

Using cream yarn,

R1   6 sc in magic ring. **(6 sts)**

R2   Inc in each st around. **(12 sts)**

R3   *Sc 1, inc* 6 times. **(18 sts)**

R4-6 Sc 18.

R7   *Sc 1, inv dec* 6 times. **(12 sts)**

Add the 6mm safety eyes, placing them between rounds 5 and 6, about 2 stitches apart. Sew on the mouth. *(photo 41)*

41

R8   In FLO, *3 hdc, sl st* 6 times. *(photo 42)*

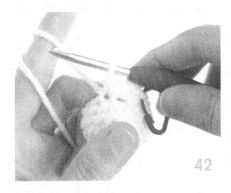

42

Begin adding fiberfill and continue as you close the piece.

R9   In BLO leftover from R8, inv dec around. **(6 sts)** *(photos 43+44)*

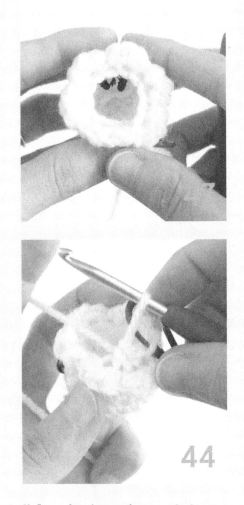

Fasten off and leave a tail for closing piece. *(photos 45+46)*

POPSiCLE

MATERIALS

- Worsted weight/4-ply yarn:
  - White, pink, or mint
  - Brown
  - Tan
- Size G/4mm crochet hook
- 1 pair of 9mm safety eyes
- Black embroidery floss
- Small embroidery needle
- Fiberfill stuffing
- Pipe cleaner, measuring 3.5 inches
- Stitch marker
- Scissors
- *Optional*: pink felt and thread for cheeks
- *Optional*: colorful embroidery floss or yarn for sprinkles

ABBREVIATIONS

BLO	Back Loops Only
CH	Chain
DC	Double Crochet
HDC	Half Double Crochet

INC	Increase
INV DEC	Invisible Decrease
R	Round or Row
SC	Single Crochet
SL ST	Slip Stitch
ST/S	Stitch/es

FINISHED MEASUREMENTS

POPSICLE

approx. 2 inches wide by 5.5 inches tall

POPSICLE

Using *mint*, *pink*, or _____,

R1   6 sc in magic ring. **(6 sts)**

R2   Inc in each st around. **(12 sts)**

R3   *Sc 1, inc* 6 times. **(18 sts)**

R4   *Sc 2, inc* 6 times. **(24 sts)**

R5-21 Sc 24.

Add the safety eyes, placing them between rounds 15 and 16, about 4 stitches apart. Sew on the mouth. Add felt cheeks. *(photo 1)*

R2

2   In BLO *Sc 2, inv dec* 6 times. **(18 sts)** *(photo 2)*

Begin adding fiberfill and continue as you close the piece.

R2
3   *Sc 1, inv dec* 6 times. **(12 sts)**

R2
4   Inv dec around 6 times. **(6 sts)**

Fasten off and leave a tail for closing the piece. *(photo 3)*

3

STiCK

Using *tan yarn*,

R1   7 sc in magic ring. **(7 sts)**

R2-8 Sc 7.

Fasten off and leave a tail for sewing.

Insert the pipe cleaner into the stick. *(photo 4)* A little will stick out the end, and that's okay! Insert the remaining pipe cleaner into R24 of the popsicle. *(photo 5)* With the yarn needle, sew the stick to the popsicle. Secure and hide the tail. *(photos 6+7)*

4

6

7

NOTE: For safety, if giving this to small children, fold the tip of the pipe cleaner about half an inch before inserting it into the stick piece. This way the pipe cleaner doesn't accidentally poke out the stick while being played with.

CHOCOLATE SHELL

Using **brown yarn**,

R1   6 sc in magic ring. **(6 sts)**

R2   Inc in each st around. **(12 sts)**

R3   *Sc 1, inc* 6 times. **(18 sts)**

R4   *Sc 2, inc* 6 times. **(24 sts)**

R5-9 Sc 24.

This next round will form the dripping parts of the chocolate. After each drip is made, make sure to sl st back into the same space as the sc that was made before beginning the chain.

Sc 2, sc hdc, 2 dc, hdc sc, sc 3, ch 5 and starting in the 2nd ch from hook hdc across 4 times. Sl st back into the same space as the sc that was made before beginning the chain. *(photos 8-10)* Sc 2, hdc dc, dc hdc, sc 4, hdc dc, dc hdc, sc 3, ch 8 and starting in the 2nd ch from hook hdc across 7 times. Sl st back into the same space as the sc. Sc 3. *(photo 11)*

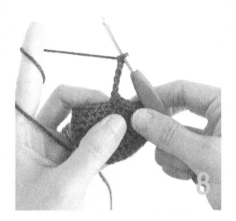

Fasten off and leave a long tail for sewing. With the yarn needle, sew the chocolate onto the popsicle. Make sure to weave the needle through the stitches from R10 and not over them. *(photos 12+13)* This will give the popsicle a clean finish. Secure and hide the tail. *(photos 14+15)*

Optional: Make one without the chocolate and use colorful embroidery floss for sprinkles! *(photos 16+17)*

16

17

DINNER

BURGER & FRIES

MATERIALS

✖ Worsted weight/4-ply yarn:
  - Tan
  - Cream
  - Brown
  - Yellow
  - Red
  - Green
  - Golden yellow

✖ Size F/3.75mm crochet hook

✖ 2 pairs of 9mm safety eyes

✖ Black embroidery floss

✖ Small embroidery needle

✖ Fiberfill stuffing

✖ Yarn needle

✖ Stitch marker

✖ Scissors

✖ Thin cardboard

ABBREVIATIONS

CH	Chain
DC	Double Crochet

HDC	Half Double Crochet
INC	Increase
INV DEC	Invisible Decrease
R	Round or Row
SC	Single Crochet
SK	Skip
SL ST	Slip Stitch
ST/S	Stitch/es

FINISHED MEASUREMENTS

BURGER

approx. 3 inches wide by 3.5 inches tall

FRY CONTAINER

approx. 3 inches wide by 2 inches tall

FRIES

approx. 0.5 inches wide by 3 inches tall

INSIDE BUN

MAKE 2

Using ground yarn,

R1   6 sc in magic ring. **(6 sts)**

R2   Inc in each st around. **(12 sts)**

R3   *Sc 1, inc* 6 times. **(18 sts)**

R4   *Inc, sc 2* 6 times. **(24 sts)**

R5   *Sc 3, inc* 6 times. **(30 sts)**

R6   *Inc, sc 4* 6 times. **(36 sts)**

R7   *Sc 5, inc* 6 times. **(42 sts)**

R8   *Inc, sc 6* 6 times. **(48 sts)**

Fasten off and leave a long tail for sewing. *(photo 1)*

1

Trace the pieces onto thin cardboard and cut them out. You'll want the cardboard to be slightly smaller than the crochet piece. *(photo 2)* Set aside.

2

TOP BUN

Using *tan yarn*,

R1   6 sc in magic ring. **(6 sts)**

R2   Inc in each st around. **(12 sts)**

R3   *Sc 1, inc* 6 times. **(18 sts)**

R4   *Sc 2, inc* 6 times. **(24 sts)**

R5   *Sc 3, inc* 6 times. **(30 sts)**

R6   *Sc 4, inc* 6 times. **(36 sts)**

R7   *Sc 5, inc* 6 times. **(42 sts)**

R8   *Sc 6, inc* 6 times. **(48 sts)**

R9-12 Sc 48.

Fasten off and weave in the ends. Add the safety eyes, placing them between rounds 10 and 11, about 4 stitches apart. Sew on the mouth. *(photo 3)* Using cream yarn, sew sesame seeds on the top of the bun. *(photo 4)*

3

4

TO ASSEMBLE THE TOP BUN

Use a yarn needle to sew one of the inside bun pieces to the top bun piece. Make sure to weave the needle through the back loops of R12 on the top bun piece and R8 on the inside bun piece. *(photos 5+6)* Be sure to weave the needle through the stitches, not over them, to create a clean finish on the bun. Once you are a little more than halfway around, while there is still space to insert cardboard and fiberfill, insert the cardboard piece. *(photo 7)* Then add fiberfill on top of the cardboard, filling only the top part of the bun. Secure and hide the tail. *(photo 8)*

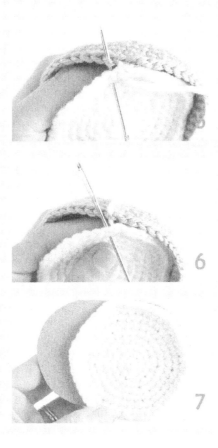

6

7

BOTTOM BUN

Using *tan yarn*,

R1 6 sc in magic ring. **(6 sts)**

R2 Inc in each st around. **(12 sts)**

R3 *Sc 1, inc* 6 times. **(18 sts)**

R4 *Sc 2, inc* 6 times. **(24 sts)**

R5 *Sc 3, inc* 6 times. **(30 sts)**

R6 *Sc 4, inc* 6 times. **(36 sts)**

R7 *Sc 5, inc* 6 times. **(42 sts)**

R8 *Sc 6, inc* 6 times. **(48 sts)**

R9+10 Sc 48.

Fasten off and weave in the ends. *(photo 9)* Sew the remaining inside bun piece to the bottom bun piece, following the same technique for sewing the top bun pieces together. Weave the needle through the back loops of R10 on the bottom bun piece and R8 on the inside bun piece. *(photos 10+11)* Once you are a little more than halfway around, while there is still space to insert cardboard and fiberfill, insert the cardboard piece. Then add fiberfill on top of the cardboard, filling only the bottom part of the bun. Secure and hide the tail. *(photos 12+13)*

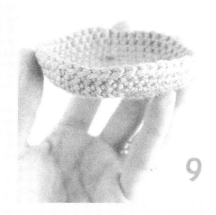

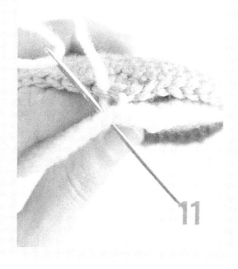

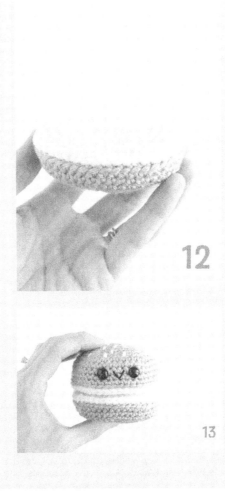

12

13

PATTY

Using **brown yam**,

R1	6 sc in magic ring. **(6 sts)**
R2	Inc in each st around. **(12 sts)**
R3	*Sc 1, inc* 6 times. **(18 sts)**
R4	*Sc 2, inc* 6 times. **(24 sts)**
R5	*Sc 3, inc* 6 times. **(30 sts)**
R6	*Sc 4, inc* 6 times. **(36 sts)**
R7	*Sc 5, inc* 6 times. **(42 sts)**
R8	*Sc 6, inc* 6 times. **(48 sts)**
R9	Sc 48.

Sc 6, inv dec 6 times. **(42 sts)**

Sc 5, inv dec 6 times. **(36 sts)**

Sc 4, inv dec 6 times. **(30 sts)**

Sc 3, inv dec 6 times. **(24 sts)**

Sc 2, inv dec 6 times. **(18 sts)**

Sc 1, inv dec 6 times. **(12 sts)**

Inv dec around 6 times. **(6 sts)**

Fasten off and leave a tail for closing the piece. Leave the patty unstuffed. *(photos 14+15)*

14

15

CHEESE

Using yellow yarn, Ch 14.

R1 Starting in 2nd ch from hook sc across. **(13 sts)** Ch 1 and turn.

R2-13 Sc 13. Ch 1 and turn. Do not ch 1 and turn after row 13.

R14 Sc around three edges. To do this, begin by placing a sc into the same space as the last sc you just made. *(photo 16)* This will help turn the work so you can work along the sides. Sc 11, then inc in the corner space. *(photo 17)* Sc 11 across, then inc in the corner space once more. Sc 11, then sc into the fourth corner. This acts as an increase in the corner. You should have 52 sts at the end.

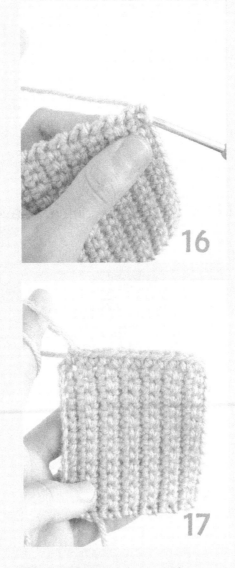

Fasten off and weave in the ends. *(photo 18)*

18

LETTUCE

Using *green yarn*,

R1 6 sc in magic ring. **(6 sts)**

R2 Inc in each st around. **(12 sts)**

R3 *Sc 1, inc* 6 times. **(18 sts)**

R4 *Sc 2, inc* 6 times. **(24 sts)**

R5 *Sc 3, inc* 6 times. **(30 sts)**

R6 *Sc 4, inc* 6 times. **(36 sts)**

R7 *Sc, 2 hdc, 2 dc, 2 hdc* 9 times. **(63 sts)**

Fasten off and weave in the ends. *(photo 19)*

19

TOMATO

Using *red yarn*,

R1   6 sc in magic ring. **(6 sts)**

R2   Inc in each st around. **(12 sts)**

R3   *Sc 1, inc* 6 times. **(18 sts)**

R4   Ch 2, dc, *Ch 2, sk 1 st, 2 dc in 1 st* 8 times. *(photos 20–24)* Ch 2, sk the last st and sl st into the 2nd ch from the very beginning of the round. **(36 sts)** *Note: Sl st will count as a st!* *(photos 25–27)*

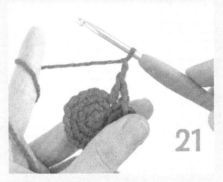

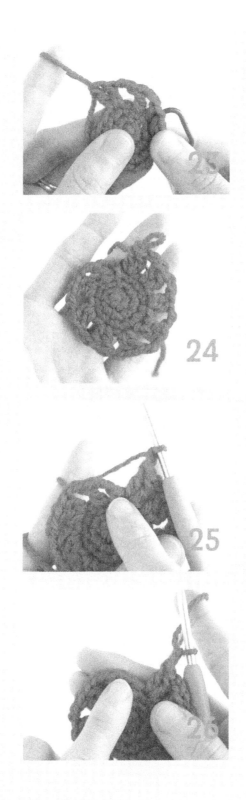

R5 Ch 1, sc 36, sl st into ch 1. **(36 sts)**

Fasten off and weave in the ends. *(photo 28)*

28

Stack all the ingredients—lettuce, tomato, patty, cheese—and place between buns. If you want the pieces to be sewn together, just use yarn and a yarn needle to sew them together. *(photo 29)*

29

FRY COUNTAINER

Using *red yarn*, Ch 16.

In the next row, go through both loops, leaving the back "bump." *(photos 30–32)*

30

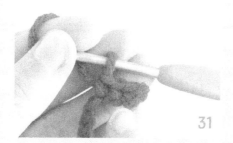

31

32

R1 Starting in 2nd ch from hook sc across 15 times, turn and sc across 15 times in the back "bumps." **(30 sts)** *(photos 33+34)*

33

34

R2-11 Sc 30.

Fasten off and weave in the ends. Add the safety eyes, placing them between rounds 6 and 7, about 3 stitches apart. Sew on the mouth. *(photos 35–38)*

35

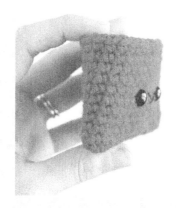

36

37

38

FRIES

MAKE 10

Using golden yellow yarn, Ch 15.

R1   Starting in 2nd ch from hook hdc across. **(14 sts)**

Fasten off and weave in the ends. *(photo 39)*

39

Tuck the fries into the container. *(photos 40+41)*

40

41

CHINESE TAKEOUT: SHRIMP LO MEIN & FORTUNE COOKIE

MATERIALS

- Worsted weight/4-ply yarn:
  - White
  - Light tan
  - Peach
  - Red
  - Dark tan

- Size G/4mm crochet hook

- 1 pair of 9mm safety eyes for the container

- 3 pairs of 6mm eyes for the shrimp and fortune cookie

- Black embroidery floss

- Small embroidery needle

- Fiberfill stuffing

- Yarn needle

- Stitch markers (four to five, for assembling the sides)

- Scissors

- White felt

- 2 pipe cleaner pieces, each measuring 5 inches

ABBREVIATIONS

| BLO | Back Loops Only |

CH	Chain
INC	Increase
INV DEC	Invisible Decrease
R	Round or Row
SC	Single Crochet
ST/S	Stitch/es

FINISHED MEASUREMENTS

CONTAINER

approx. 2.75 inches wide by 3.25 inches long by 2.75 inches tall

SHRIMP

approx. 1 inch wide by 2.5 inches tall

FORTUNE COOKIE

approx. 2.25 inches wide by 2.25 inches tall

CHOPSTICKS

approx. 0.5 inches wide by 5 inches tall

TAKEOUT CONTAINER

BASE

Using _____ , Ch 15.

R1   Starting in 2nd ch from hook sc across. **(14 sts)** Ch 1 and turn.

R2-12 Sc 14. Ch 1 and turn. Do not ch 1 and turn after row 12.

R1

3   Sc around the three edges. To do this, begin by placing a sc into the same space as the last sc you just made. *(photo 1)* This will help turn the work so you can work along the sides. Sc 10, then inc in the corner space. *(photo 2)* Sc 12 across, then inc in the corner space once more. *(photo 3)* Sc 10, then sc into the fourth corner. This acts as an increase in the corner. *(photo 4)* Ch 1. You should have 52 sts at the end. Keep in mind that the ch 1 does not count as a stitch!

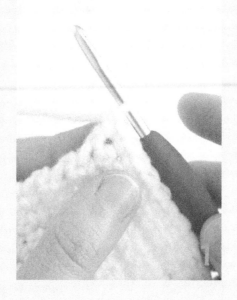

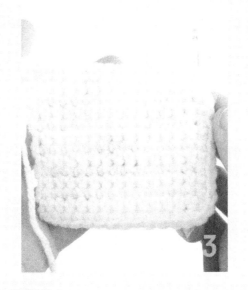

R1
4   In BLO, Sc 52. *(photo 5)*

5

The next rounds will be worked in a continuous spiral. Do not join work.

R15-24 Sc 52.

R2
5   Sc 52, then sc 3. The extra stitches help even out the piece.

Fasten off and weave in the ends. Add the 9mm safety eyes, placing them between rows 19 and 20, about 4 stitches apart. Sew on the mouth. *(photo 6)*

6

To give the container angled corners, simply hold the outside corners with your thumb and index finger while pushing with your middle finger from inside the container. *(photos 7+8)*

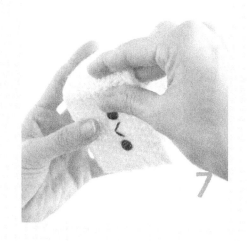

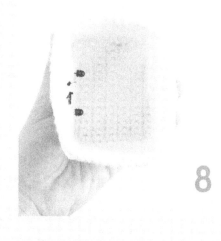

FRONT/BACK FLAPS

MAKE 2

Using _____, Ch 15.

R1 Starting in 2nd ch from hook sc across. **(14 sts)** Ch 1 and turn.

R2-7 Sc 14. Ch 1 and turn. Do not ch 1 and turn after row 7.

Fasten off and leave a tail for sewing. *(photo 9)*

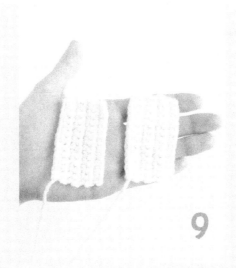

9

SIDE FLAPS

MAKE 2

Using ＿＿＿＿＿＿＿, Ch 13.

R1   Starting in 2nd ch from hook sc across. **(12 sts)** Ch 1 and turn.

R2-7 Sc 12. Ch 1 and turn. Do not ch 1 and turn after row 7.

Fasten off and leave a tail for sewing. *(photo 10)*

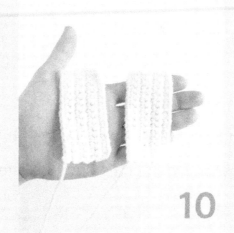

10

1 On the last single crochet from R25 of the container, place a stitch marker. This will count as stitch 1. Now count a total of 12 stitches along the shorter side and place another stitch marker. *(photo 11)*

2 Counting from the stitch next to the twelfth stitch, count a total of 14 stitches across the front side of the container (the side with the safety eyes). In the fifteenth stitch, place another stitch marker. Now count a total of 12 stitches along the shorter side again and place a stitch marker. You will have four stitch markers in total, with the sides containing 12 stitches and the front and back sides containing 14 stitches. *(photo 12)*

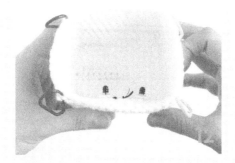

3 Line up a side flap with the stitch makers. *(photo 13)* Remember, the stitches with stitch markers are part of the 12 stitches, so line the flap up evenly with the container.

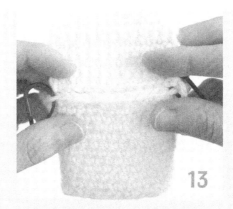

13

4 Bring the yarn needle down through the stitch that has the marker. Then weave it back up through the last stitch on the flap. *(photos 14+15)* Continue doing this technique until you reach the end. Your side flap should look like *photo 16* once completely attached. Secure and weave in the end.

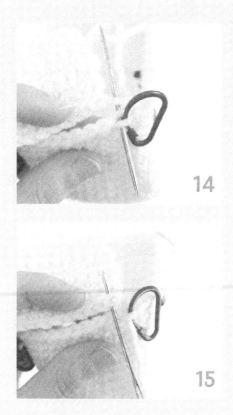

14

15

5 Repeat steps 3 and 4 for the other side flap. *(photo 17)*

6 For the front flap, count the 14 remaining stitches along the front of the container. Place the stitch markers in the corners to indicate where the flap should line up. *(photos 18+19)*

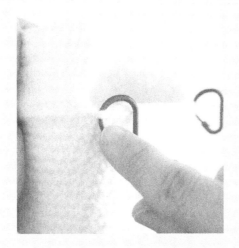

7 Line up the front flap with the stitch markers. *(photo 20)* Remember, the stitches with the stitch markers are part of the 14 stitches, so line the flap up evenly with the container.

8 Repeat step 4 to sew the flap to the container. *(photos 21+22)*

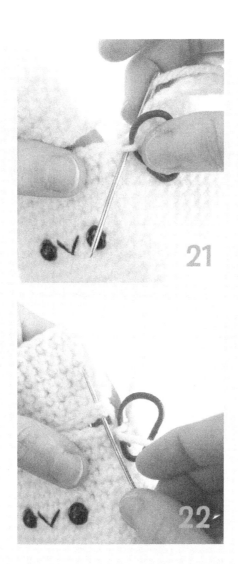

9 Then repeat steps 6-8 to sew the back flap to the container. *(photos 23+24)*

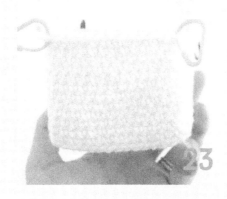

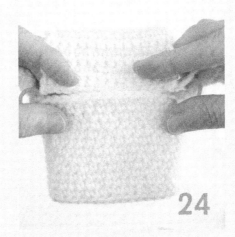

24

10 Make sure to secure and weave in all ends. *(photos 25–27)*

25

26

27

NOODLES

MAKE 4

Using *light tan yarn*,

Ch 300 OR chain until piece measures 64 inches.

Use stitch markers to mark every 50 or 100 chains for easy counting! *(photo 28)*

28

Fasten off and weave in the ends.

TO ASSEMBLE THE NOODLES

Wrap one noodle strand around four fingers and gently pull it off. *(photos 29+30)* Repeat for all four strands. *(photo 31)* Place the four bundles in the container. *(photo 32)*

32

BODY

MAKE 2

Using *peach yarn*,

R1   6 sc in magic ring. **(6 sts)**

R2   Inc in each st around. **(12 sts)**

R3   *Sc 1, inc* 6 times. **(18 sts)**

R4   *Sc 1, inv dec* 6 times. **(12 sts)**

R5-11 Sc 12.

Add the 6mm safety eyes, placing them between rounds 5 and 6, about 2 stitches apart. Sew on the mouth. Add fiberfill.

R1
2   Inv dec around 6 times. **(6 sts)**

Fasten off and leave a tail for the closing piece. *(photo 33)*

TAIL

MAKE 2

Using *red yarn*, Ch 14.

Fasten off and leave a tail for sewing. *(photo 34)*

34

TO MAKE THE TAIL

1 Holding both ends in one hand, use the other hand to push the middle of the tail to form a "W." *(photos 35+36)*

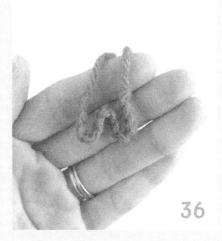

36

2 With the yarn needle, weave through the middle and other end of the tail and pull through. *(photos 37-39)*

37

3 Sew the tail to the bottom of the shrimp. Secure and hide the yarn tail.
(photos 40+41)

40

41

Place the shrimps in the container with the noodles. *(photo 42)*

42

CHOPSTICKS

MAKE 2

Using *red yarn*,

R1   Sc 5 in magic ring. **(5 sts)**

R2-5 Sc 5.

Change to *dark tan yarn*,

R6-21 Sc 5.

Insert the pipe cleaner into the chopstick. Fasten off and leave a tail for closing the piece. *(photo 43)* Place the chopsticks in the container. *(photo 44)*

43

44

NOTE: For safety, if giving this to small children, fold the tips of the pipe cleaner about half an inch before inserting it into the chopstick piece. This way the pipe cleaner doesn't accidentally poke out while the chopsticks are being played with.

FORTUNE COOKIE

Using *dark tan yarn*,

R1 6 sc in magic ring. **(6 sts)**

R2 Inc in each st around. **(12 sts)**

R3 *Sc 1, inc* 6 times. **(18 sts)**

R4 *Inc, sc 2* 6 times. **(24 sts)**

R5 *Sc 3, inc* 6 times. **(30 sts)**

R6 *Inc, sc 4* 6 times. **(36 sts)**

R7 *Sc 5, inc* 6 times. **(42 sts)**

R8 *Inc, sc 6* 6 times. **(48 sts)**

R9 *Sc 7, inc* 6 times. **(54 sts)**

Fasten off and leave a tail for sewing. Add the 6mm safety eyes, placing them between rounds 6 and 7, about 2 stitches apart. Use *photo 45* as a reference where to place the eyes (notice where the blue stitch marker is). Sew on the mouth. *(photo 45)*

45

1 Fold the fortune cookie in half. *(photo 46)*

46

2 With the yarn needle, weave through the top of the stitches of R9. *(photos 47+48)* Make sure to weave the needle through the stitches, not over them, to create a clean finish on the outside edge of the cookie. *(photo 49)*

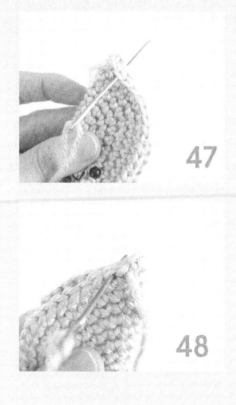

47

48

3 About halfway through, begin adding fiberfill. *(photo 50)* Continue to add fiberfill as you sew the cookie closed.

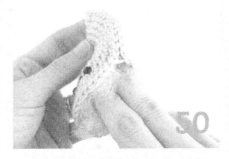

4 Cut a small rectangle out of white felt for the fortune. *(photo 51)* Once there are about 6 stitches left to sew, insert the felt into the cookie, leaving a little sticking out. *(photo 52)* Continue sewing the cookie closed, going through the felt as you work. *(photo 53)*

53

5 Before securing and hiding the yarn tail, press the two corner ends together. *(photo 54)* This will help form the shape of the fortune cookie.

54

6 Weave the needle through to the middle of the cookie, where the magic ring is. Sew the inner sides together so the shape holds. *(photo 55)* Secure and hide the tail. *(photo 56)*

55

56

LOBSTER & CORN ON THE COB

MATERIALS

- Worsted weight/4-ply yarn:
  - Red
  - White
  - Light yellow
  - Green

- Size F/3.75mm crochet hook

- 2 pairs of 6mm eyes for the lobster and butter dish

- 1 pair of 9mm safety eyes for the corn on the cob

- Black embroidery floss

- Small embroidery needle

- Fiberfill stuffing

- Yarn needle

- Stitch marker

- Scissors

- Straight pins (helpful when assembling pieces)

ABBREVIATIONS

BLO	Back Loops Only
CH	Chain
DC	Double Crochet

DEC	Decrease
	(this is not the same as an invisible decrease!)
FLO	Front Loops Only
HDC	Half Double Crochet
INC	Increase
INV DEC	Invisible Decrease
R	Round or Row
SC	Single Crochet
SL ST	Slip Stitch
ST/S	Stitch/es
TR	Treble Crochet

FINISHED MEASUREMENTS

LOBSTER

approx. 6 inches wide by 7 inches long by 1.5 inches tall

BUTTER DISH

approx. 2 inches wide by 1.25 inches tall

CORN ON THE COB

approx. 2.5 inches wide by 5 inches tall

BODY

Using *red yarn*,

R1   6 sc in magic ring. **(6 sts)**

R2   Sc 6.

R3   Inc in each st around. **(12 sts)**

R4   *Sc 1, inc* 6 times. **(18 sts)**

R5   Sc 18.

R6   *Sc 2, inc* 6 times. **(24 sts)**

Add the 6mm safety eyes, placing them between rounds 4 and 5, about 3 stitches apart. ***Note:** Placement of the eyes is key here. Before inserting them, make sure your stitch marker/end of round is on the RIGHT side. When we work R28, you'll want the ruffles to be in the center and this helps ensure they're in the correct place.*

R7   Sc 24.

R8   *Sc 3, inc* 6 times. **(30 sts)**

R9-11   Sc 30.

Begin adding fiberfill and continue as you go.

R1
2   *Sc 3, inv dec* 6 times. **(24 sts)**

R13-26 Sc 24.

R2
7   *Sc 2, inv dec* 6 times. **(18 sts)** *(photo 1)*

This next round will form the ruffles on the tail. Each comma represents a move to the next ch space.

R2
8   Sc in the next 7 sts, *1 hdc and 2 dc in one st, 2 tr in one st, 2 dc and 1 hdc in one st* 3 times. Sc in the next 2 sts. **(33 sts)** *(photos 2–6)*

Fasten off and leave a tail for sewing. To close the lobster body, weave the needle through the top of the stitches of **R28** and right below the "ruffle" part. *(photos 7+8)*

TAiL

MAKE 3

Using *red yarn,* Ch 12.

In the next row, go through both loops, leaving the back "bump."

R1   Starting in 2nd ch from hook sc across. **(11 sts)**

Fasten off and leave a tail for sewing. *(photo 9)*

Pin the tail pieces to the back, near the ruffles. Sew into place, only sewing the ends of the strips. *(photo 10)* Secure and hide the yarn tail. *(photo 11)*

ANTENNA

MAKE 2

Using *red yarn*, Ch 12.

R1   Starting in 2nd ch from hook sl st across. **(11 sts)**

Fasten off and leave a tail for sewing. *(photo 12)*

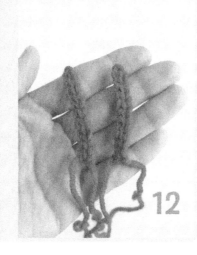

With the yarn needle, sew the antennas to the tip of the body on the sides of the magic ring. Secure and hide the tail. *(photo 13)*

LARGE LEG PiECE

MAKE 2

Using *red yarn,*

R1   5 sc in magic ring. **(5 sts)**

R2   Inc in each st around. **(10 sts)**

R3   In BLO, Sc 10.

R4-6   Sc 10.

Fasten off and leave a tail for sewing.

Add fiberfill. Set aside. *(photo 14)*

SMALL LEG PiECE

MAKE 2

Using *red yarn*,

R1   6 sc in magic ring. **(6 sts)**

R2   In BLO, Sc 6.

R3   Sc 6.

R4   *Sc 1, inc* 3 times. **(9 sts)**

Fasten off and leave a tail for sewing. Add a little bit of fiberfill. Set aside.
(photo 15)

BiG CLAW

MAKE 2

Using *red yarn*,

R1   6 sc in magic ring. **(6 sts)**

R2   Sc 6.

R3   *Sc 1, inc* 3 times. **(9 sts)**

R4 Sc 9.

R5 *Sc 2, inc* 3 times. **(12 sts)**

R6 Sc 12.

R7 *Sc 3, inc* 3 times. **(15 sts)**

R8 *Sc 4, inc* 3 times. **(18 sts)**

Begin adding fiberfill and continue as you close the piece.

R9 *Sc 1, inv dec* 6 times. **(12 sts)**

**R1
0** Inv dec around 6 times. **(6 sts)**

Fasten off and leave a tail for closing the piece. Set aside. *(photo 16)*

16

SMALL CLAW

MAKE 2

Using *red yarn*,

R1 6 sc in magic ring. **(6 sts)**

R2 Sc 6.

R3 *Sc 1, inc* 3 times. **(9 sts)**

R4+5   Sc 9.

Fasten off and leave a tail for sewing. Add a little bit of fiberfill. Set aside. *(photo 17)*

17

TO ASSEMBLE THE LEGS

With the yarn needle, sew the open end of the small leg piece to the large leg piece. *(photo 18)* Make sure to sew the leg at a slight angle to help the leg curve. Next, sew the big claw to the large leg piece, sewing at an angle again. *(photo 19)* Sew the small claw to the big claw near the middle, where the leg and big claw meet. *(photo 20)* Secure and hide the tails. *(photo 21)* Finally, cut a length of red yarn long enough for sewing. Use this to sew the legs to the body of the lobster. Make sure to position the legs so they are near rounds 8-10 of the body. *(photos 22+23)*

18

19

20

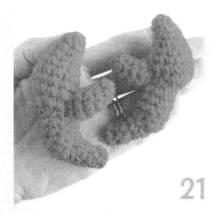

21

WALKING LEGS

MAKE 8

Using *red yarn*, Ch 8.

R1   Starting in 2nd ch from hook sl st across. **(7 sts)**

Fasten off and leave a tail for sewing. *(photo 24)*

With the yarn needle, sew four walking legs on each side of the body. *(photo 25)* Make sure to place them starting right after the larger legs. *(photo 26)* Secure and hide the tail. *(photo 27)*

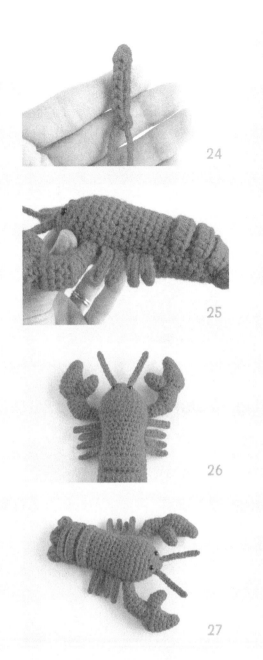

24

25

26

27

BUTTER

Using *light yellow yarn*,

R1   6 sc in magic ring. **(6 sts)**

R2   Inc in each st around. **(12 sts)**

R3   *Sc 1, inc* 6 times. **(18 sts)**

R4   *Inc, sc 2* 6 times. **(24 sts)**

Fasten off and leave a tail for sewing. *(photo 28)*

28

DiSH

Using   ,

R1   6 sc in magic ring. **(6 sts)**

R2   Inc in each st around. **(12 sts)**

R3   *Sc 1, inc* 6 times. **(18 sts)**

R4   *Inc, sc 2* 6 times. **(24 sts)**

R5   *Sc 3, inc* 6 times. **(30 sts)**

R6   In BLO, Sc 30.

R7-9   Sc 30.

R10   In FLO, Sc 30.

Fasten off and weave in the ends. Add the 6mm safety eyes, placing them between rounds 7 and 8, about 2 stitches apart. Sew on the mouth. *(photo 29)*

29

With the yarn needle, sew the butter to the dish. Weave the needle through the back loops leftover from R10 of the dish and R4 of the butter. *(photos 30+31)* The butter will fit snugly inside the dish, even though the butter only has 24 sts and the dish has 30 sts. Make sure the butter is flat and not bunching. Add fiberfill before closing piece. Secure and hide the tail. *(photo 32)*

30

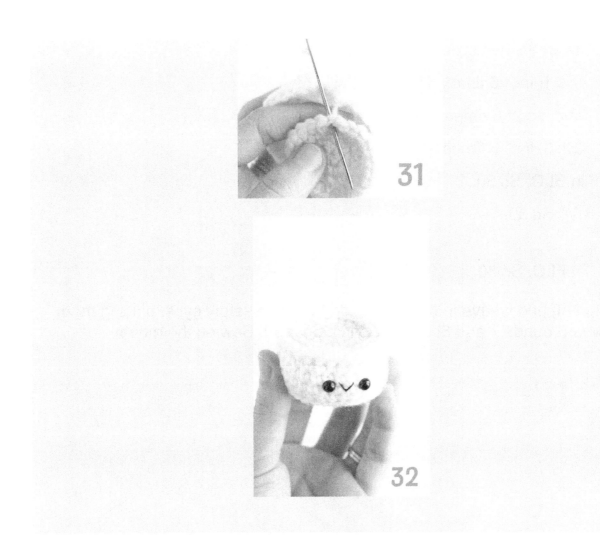

31

32

CORN

Using *light yellow yarn*,

R1 6 sc in magic ring. **(6 sts)**

R2 Inc in each st around. **(12 sts)**

R3 *Sc 1, inc* 6 times. **(18 sts)**

R4 *Sc 2, inc* 6 times. **(24 sts)**

R5+6 Sc 24.

R7 *Sc 3, inc* 6 times. **(30 sts)**

R8-23 Sc 30.

Add the 9mm safety eyes, placing them between rounds 14 and 15, about 4 stitches apart. Sew on the mouth. Begin adding fiberfill and continue as you go.

R24 *Sc 3, inv dec* 6 times. **(24 sts)**

R25 *Sc 2, inv dec* 6 times. **(18 sts)**

R26 *Sc 1, inv dec* 6 times. **(12 sts)**

R27 Inv dec around 6 times. **(6 sts)**

Fasten off and leave a tail for closing the piece. *(photo 33)*

33

HUSK

Using *green yarn*,

R1   6 sc in magic ring. **(6 sts)**

R2   Inc in each st around. **(12 sts)**

R3   *Sc 1, inc* 6 times. **(18 sts)**

R4   *Sc 2, inc* 6 times. **(24 sts)**

R5   *Sc 3, inc* 6 times. **(30 sts)**

R6   *Sc 4, inc* 6 times. **(36 sts)**

R7-13   Sc 36.

These next rounds will form the sides of the husks. *(photos 34–37)*

R1
4   Sc 18. Ch 1 and turn.

R1
5   Dec, sc 14, dec. **(16 sts)** Ch 1 and turn.

R1
6   Sc 16. Ch 1 and turn.

R1
7   Dec, sc 12, dec. **(14 sts)** Ch 1 and turn.

R18 Sc 14. Ch 1 and turn.

R19 Dec, sc 10, dec. **(12 sts)** Ch 1 and turn.

R20 Sc 12. Ch 1 and turn.

R21 Dec, sc 8, dec. **(10 sts)** Ch 1 and turn.

R22 Sc 10. Ch 1 and turn.

R23 Dec, sc 6, dec. **(8 sts)** Ch 1 and turn.

R24 Sc 8. Ch 1 and turn.

R25 Dec, sc 4, dec. **(6 sts)** Ch 1 and turn.

R26 Sc 6. Ch 1 and turn.

R27 Dec, sc 2, dec. **(4 sts)** Ch 1 and turn.

R28 Dec 2 times. **(2 sts)** Ch 1 and turn.

R29 Dec 1 time. **(1 st)**

Fasten off and weave in the end. *(photos 38+39)*

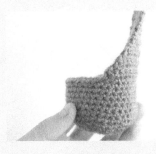

38

For the second side of the husk, join the yarn in the 18th st. *(photos 40–42)* Ch 1 (this does not count as a stitch). *(photo 43)* Then, repeat R14–29. *(photos 44+45)* Fasten off and weave in the ends. *(photo 46)*

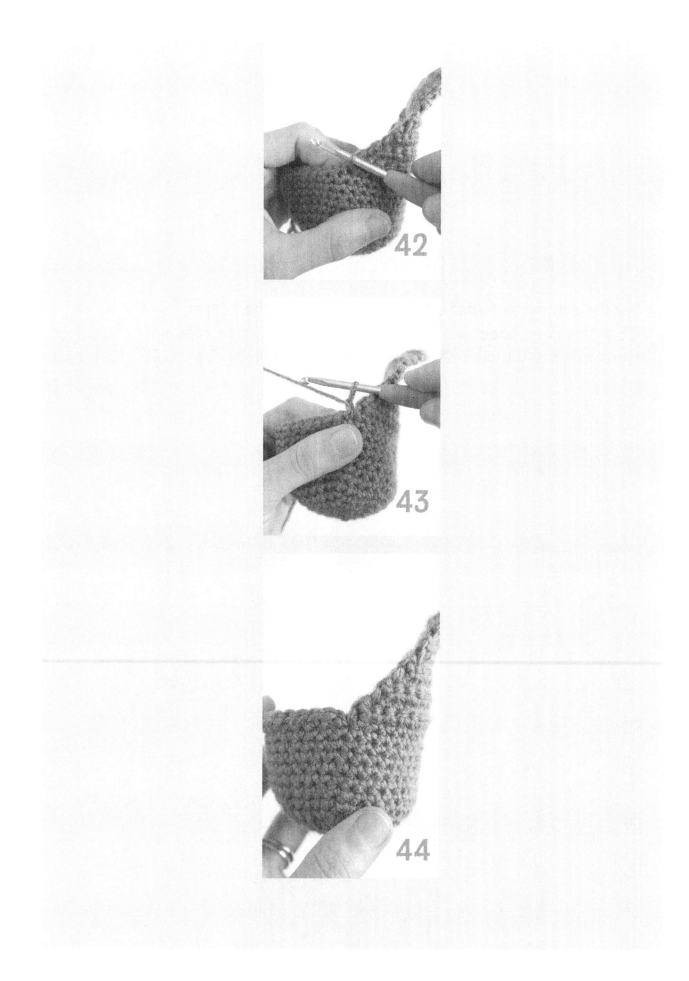

45

46

STALK

Using *green yarn*,

R1   6 sc in magic ring. **(6 sts)**

R2   Inc in each st around. **(12 sts)**

433

R3 In BLO, Sc 12.

R4 Sc 12.

Fasten off and leave a tail for sewing. Add a little bit of fiberfill. *(photo 47)*
With the yarn needle, sew the stalk to the bottom of the husk. *(photo 48)*
Secure and hide the tail. Add the corn to the husk. *(photos 49+50)*

49

50

PIZZA

MATERIALS

- Worsted weight/4-ply yarn:
  - Tan
  - Dark red
  - Cream
  - Green
  - White
  - Burgundy
  - Brown

- Size F/3.75mm crochet hook

- 1 pair of 6mm safety eyes

- Black embroidery floss

- Small embroidery needle

- Yarn needle

- Stitch marker

- Scissors

ABBREVIATIONS

CH	Chain
DEC	Decrease
	(this is not the same as an invisible decrease!)
HDC	Half Double Crochet
INC	Increase

R	Round or Row
SC	Single Crochet
SL ST	Slip Stitch
ST/S	Stitch/es

FINISHED MEASUREMENTS

PIZZA

approx. 4 inches wide by 5 inches long

CRUST

Using *tan yarn*, Ch 19.

In the next row, go through both loops, leaving the back "bump." *(photos 1+2)*

R1   Starting in 2nd ch from hook sc across. **(18 sts)** Ch 1 and turn.

R2-9   Sc 18. Ch 1 and turn. *(photo 3)*

This next row will form the crust.

R1
0   Fold the piece over and line up the "bumps" with the stitches from R9, then sc into both the bumps and the stitches. Ch 1 and turn. *(photos 4–7)*

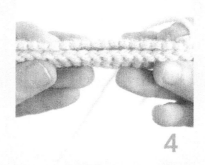

4

5

6

R11-13 Sc 18. Ch 1 and turn. *(photos 8+9)*

R1
4 Dec, sc 14, dec. **(16 sts)** Ch 1 and turn.

R15+1
6 Sc 16. Ch 1 and turn.

R1
7 Dec, sc 12, dec. **(14 sts)** Ch 1 and turn.

R18+1
9 Sc 14. Ch 1 and turn.

R2
0 Dec, sc 10, dec. **(12 sts)** Ch 1 and turn.

R2
1 Sc 12. Ch 1 and turn.

R2
2 Dec, sc 8, dec. **(10 sts)** Ch 1 and turn.

R23+2
4 Sc 10. Ch 1 and turn.

R25 Dec, sc 6, dec. **(8 sts)** Ch 1 and turn.

R26 Sc 8. Ch 1 and turn.

R27 Dec, sc 4, dec. **(6 sts)** Ch 1 and turn.

R28 Sc 6. Ch 1 and turn.

R29 Dec, sc 2, dec. **(4 sts)** Ch 1 and turn.

R30 Sc 4. Ch 1 and turn.

R31 Dec 2 times. **(2 sts)** Ch 1 and turn.

R32 Dec 1 time. (1 st)

Fasten off and leave a long tail for sewing. *(photo 10)*

10

CHEESE & SAUCE

MAKE 2

Using *dark red* for the sauce piece and *cream* for the cheese piece, Ch 17.

In the next row, go through both loops, leaving the back "bump."

R1 Starting in 2nd ch from hook sc across. **(16 sts)** Ch 1 and turn.

R2+3	Sc 16. Ch 1 and turn.
R4	Dec, sc 12, dec. **(14 sts)** Ch 1 and turn.
R5+6	Sc 14. Ch 1 and turn.
R7	Dec, sc 10, dec. **(12 sts)** Ch 1 and turn.
R8	Sc 12. Ch 1 and turn.
R9	Dec, sc 8, dec. **(10 sts)** Ch 1 and turn.
R10+11	Sc 10. Ch 1 and turn.
R12	Dec, sc 6, dec. **(8 sts)** Ch 1 and turn.
R13	Sc 8. Ch 1 and turn.
R14	Dec, sc 4, dec. **(6 sts)** Ch 1 and turn.
R15	Sc 6. Ch 1 and turn.
R16	Dec, sc 2, dec. **(4 sts)** Ch 1 and turn.
R17	Sc 4. Ch 1 and turn.
R18	Dec 2 times. **(2 sts)** Ch 1 and turn.
R19	Dec 1 time. **(1 st)**

Fasten off and leave a tail on the cheese. Weave in the tail on the sauce piece. *(photo 11)* Add safety eyes, placing them between rows 10 and 11 (counting from row 1 down toward tip), about 3 stitches apart. Sew on the mouth. Make sure to attach the eyes through both the cheese and sauce pieces. *(photos 12+13)*

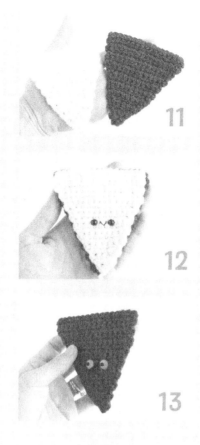

11

12

13

TO ASSEMBLE THE PiZZA

1 With the yarn needle and tail from the cheese piece, sew the cheese and sauce pieces together. Make sure to weave the needle through the two pieces and not over the stitches. *(photos 14+15)* This will create a clean edge along the sides. *(photo 16)* Continue sewing along all three edges. *(photos 17–19)* Secure and hide the tail.

14

15

2 Using the tail left over from the crust, sew the cheese and sauce pieces to the crust. Only weave the needle through the sauce and the crust. *(photos 20+21)* The stitching will be nearly invisible on the backside of the crust. *(photos 22–24)* Secure and hide the tail. *(photos 25+26)*

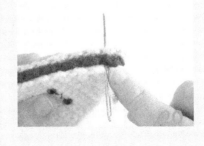

26

TOPPINGS FOR
PEPPERONI PIZZA

PEPPERONi

MAKE 3

Using **burgundy yarn,**

R1   5 sc in magic ring. **(5 sts)**

R2   Inc in each st around. **(10 sts)**

Sl st into 1st sc to fasten off. Leave a tail for sewing. *(photo 27)*

27

Sew pepperonis to the cheese. *(photo 28)*

28

SUPREME PIZZA

PEPPERS

MAKE 2

Using *green yarn*, Ch 6.

R1   Starting in 2nd ch from hook hdc across. **(5 sts)**

Fasten off and leave a tail for sewing. *(photo 29)*

29

SAUSAGE

MAKE 2

Using **brown yarn**,

R1   6 sc in magic ring. **(6 sts)**

Sl st into 1st sc to fasten off. Leave a tail for sewing. *(photo 30)*

30

MUSHROOMS

MAKE 1

Using _____ , Ch 5.

In the next row, go through both loops, leaving the back "bump." *(photo 31)*

31

R1   Starting in 2nd ch from hook, sc across 4 times, turn and sc across 4 times in the back "bumps." **(8 sts)** *(photos 32+33)*

32

R2 Inc, sc 2, inc in the next 2 sts, sc 1. *(photo 34)* Ch 4 and starting in 2nd ch from hook hdc across 3 times, sl st into the next st, inc. *(photos 35-37)*

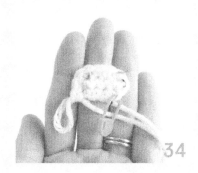

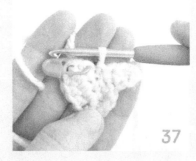

Fasten off and leave a tail for sewing. *(photo 38)*

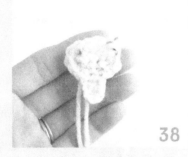

Sew the toppings in various places on top of the cheese. *(photo 39)*

SPAGHETTi MEATBALLS WiTH A GLASS OF WiNE

MATERIALS

Worsted weight/4-ply yarn:
- Cream
- Tan
- Dark red
- Brown
- Burgundy
- White

Size G/4mm crochet hook

4 pairs of 6mm eyes for the bowl and meatballs

1 pair of 9mm safety eyes for the wine glass

Black and pink embroidery floss

Small embroidery needle

Fiberfill stuffing

Yarn needle

Stitch marker

Scissors

2 pieces of pipe cleaner, each measuring 12 inches long

Thick cardboard

Straight pins (helpful when assembling the wine glass)

ABBREVIATIONS

BLO	Back Loops Only
Ch	Chain
DC	Double Crochet
HDC	Half Double Crochet
INC	Increase
INV DEC	Invisible Decrease
R	Round or Row
SC	Single Crochet
ST/S	Stitch/es

FINISHED MEASUREMENTS

BOWL

approx. 5 inches wide by 1 inch tall

MEATBALLS

approx. 1.25 inches wide by 1 inch tall

WINE GLASS

approx. 2 inches wide by 6 inches tall

SPAGHETTI

DiSH

Using cream yarn,

R1   6 sc in magic ring. **(6 sts)**

R2   Inc in each st around. **(12 sts)**

R3   *Sc 1, inc* 6 times. **(18 sts)**

R4   *Inc, sc 2* 6 times. **(24 sts)**

R5   *Sc 3, inc* 6 times. **(30 sts)**

R6   *Inc, sc 4* 6 times. **(36 sts)**

R7   In BLO, *Sc 5, inc* 6 times. **(42 sts)**

R8   *Inc, sc 6* 6 times. **(48 sts)**

R9   *Sc 7, inc* 6 times. **(54 sts)**

R10   Sc 54.

R11   *Sc 8, inc* 6 times. **(60 sts)**

R12   *Inc, sc 9* 6 times. **(66 sts)**

R13+14   Sc 66.

Fasten off and weave in the ends. Add the 6mm safety eyes, placing them between rounds 10 and 11, about 2 stitches apart. Using black embroidery floss, sew on the mouth. *(photo 1)*

SPAGHETTI NOODLES

MAKE 3

Using *tan yarn*,

Ch 300 OR chain until piece measures 64 inches.

Use stitch markers to mark every 50 or 100 chains for easy counting! *(photos 2+3)*

Fasten off and weave in the ends.

TO ASSEMBLE THE NOODLES

Wrap one strand of noodles around four fingers and gently pull it off. *(photos 4+5)*

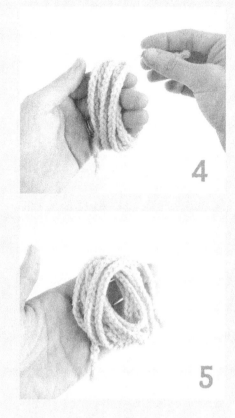

Repeat for remaining two strands. *(photo 6)*

Place the three bundles in the dish. *(photo 7)*

SAUCE

Using *dark red yarn*,

R1   6 sc in magic ring. **(6 sts)**

R2   Inc in each st around. **(12 sts)**

R3   *Sc 1, inc* 6 times. **(18 sts)**

R4   *Inc, sc 2* 6 times. **(24 sts)**

R5   *Sc 3, inc* 6 times. **(30 sts)**

This next round will form the wavy parts of the sauce.

R6   *Sc 3, hdc dc, dc hdc, sc 3, 2 hdc, 2 hdc* 3 times. **(42 sts)**

R7   Sc 42.

Fasten off and weave in the ends. *(photo 8)*

8

Using **brown yarn,**

R1   6 sc in magic ring. **(6 sts)**

R2   Inc in each st around. **(12 sts)**

R3   *Sc 1, inc* 6 times. **(18 sts)**

R4-6 Sc 18.

R7   *Sc 1, inv dec* 6 times. **(12 sts)**

Add the 6mm safety eyes, placing them between rounds 5 and 6, about 2 stitches apart. Using black embroidery floss, sew on the mouth. Begin adding fiberfill and continue as you close the piece.

R8   Inv dec around 6 times. **(6 sts)**

Fasten off and leave a tail for closing piece. *(photo 9)* Cut a length of dark red yarn, long enough to sew the meatballs to the sauce. *(photo 10)* Sew all three meatballs in place. *(photos 11+12)* Secure and hide the tail inside the meatball. Place the sauce and meatballs on top of the noodles in the dish. *(photo 13)* This will not be sewn into place. *(photos 14+15)*

9

10

11

12

13

GLASS

Using **burgundy yam**,

R1   6 sc in magic ring. **(6 sts)**

R2   Inc in each st around. **(12 sts)**

R3   *Sc 1, inc* 6 times. **(18 sts)**

R4   *Sc 2, inc* 6 times. **(24 sts)**

R5   *Sc 3, inc* 6 times. **(30 sts)**

R6   *Sc 4, inc* 6 times. **(36 sts)**

R7   Sc 36.

R8   *Sc 4, inv dec* 6 times. **(30 sts)**

R9   Sc 30.

R10   *Sc 3, inv dec* 6 times. **(24 sts)**

R11+12   Sc 24.

Change to   ,

R13-16   Sc 24.

Add the 9mm safety eyes, placing them between rounds 8 and 9, about 3 stitches apart. Using pink embroidery floss, sew on the mouth.

Fasten off and weave in the ends. *(photo 16)*

16

TOP OF GLASS

Using   ,

R1   6 sc in magic ring. **(6 sts)**

R2   Inc in each st around. **(12 sts)**

R3   *Sc 1, inc* 6 times. **(18 sts)**

R4   *Inc, sc 2* 6 times. **(24 sts)**

Fasten off and leave a tail for sewing. *(photo 17)* With the yarn needle, sew the top piece to the main wine glass. The top piece will fit snugly in the wine glass. *(photo 18)* Weave the needle through R17 of the glass and R4 of the top piece. *(photos 19+20)* Make sure to weave the needle through the stitches and not over them. This will create a clean finish on the outside of the glass. *(photo 21)* Add fiberfill before closing the piece. Secure and hide the tail. *(photo 22)*

17

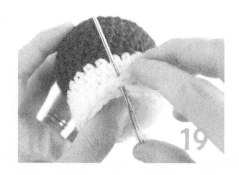

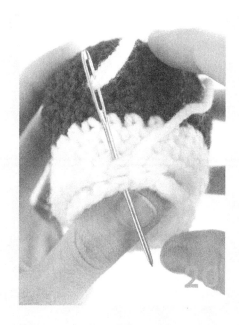

STEM

Using   ,

R1   4 sc in magic ring. **(4 sts)**

R2 Inc in each st around. **(8 sts)**

R3 In BLO, Sc 8.

R4-14 Sc 8.

Fasten off and leave a tail for sewing. *(photo 23)* Fold the two pipe cleaners into fourths and insert into the stem. *(photos 24+25)*

23

24

Trim any excess pipe cleaner that hangs out the end. It should fit completely inside the stem piece.

With a yarn needle, sew the stem to the bottom of the glass. Use straight pins to help hold the stem in place in the center. You'll want this to be as centered as possible because it supports the glass. *(photos 26+27)* Secure and hide the tail.

27

BASE

Using   ,

R1   6 sc in magic ring. **(6 sts)**

R2   Inc in each st around. **(12 sts)**

R3   *Sc 1, inc* 6 times. **(18 sts)**

R4   *Inc, sc 2* 6 times. **(24 sts)**

R5   *Sc 3, inc* 6 times. **(30 sts)**

R6   Sc 30.

Trace the base on thick cardboard and cut it out. You'll want it to be slightly smaller than the base. It should fit with a little of the base peeking out the sides. *(photo 28)* Set the cardboard aside.

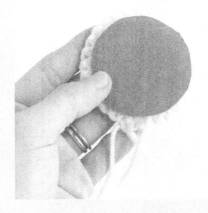

28

R7   In BLO, *Sc 3, inv dec* 6 times. **(24 sts)**

Place the cardboard inside the base and crochet the remaining rounds. No fiberfill will be added. *(photo 29)*

29

R8   *Sc 2, inv dec* 6 times. **(18 sts)**

R9   *Sc 1, inv dec* 6 times. **(12 sts)**

R1
0   Inv dec around 6 times. **(6 sts)**

Fasten off and leave a tail for closing the piece. *(photo 30)*

30

Cut a length of yarn long enough for sewing. With the yarn needle, sew the stem to the center of the base. *(photos 31+32)* Make sure the stem is centered! The thick cardboard and pipe cleaners will allow the wine glass to stand up unassisted. Secure and hide the tail. *(photo 33)*

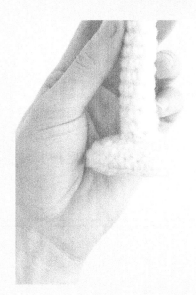

31

32

33

474

MATERIALS

✖ Worsted weight/4-ply yarn:
- Tan
- White

✖ Size G/4mm crochet hook

✖ 1 pair of 9mm safety eyes

✖ Black embroidery floss

✖ Small embroidery needle

✖ Yarn needle

✖ Stitch marker

✖ Scissors

✖ *Optional:* pink felt and thread for cheeks

ABBREVIATIONS

CH	Chain
DC	Double Crochet
HDC	Half Double Crochet
INC	Increase
R	Round or Row
SC	Single Crochet
ST/S	Stitch/es

FINISHED MEASUREMENTS

CANNOLI

approx. 5 inches long by 1.75 inches wide by 1.5 inches tall

CANNOLI

SHELL

Using *tan yarn,*

R1   6 sc in magic ring. **(6 sts)**

R2   Inc in each st around. **(12 sts)**

R3   *Sc 1, inc* 6 times. **(18 sts)**

R4   *Inc, sc 2* 6 times. **(24 sts)**

R5   *Sc 3, inc* 6 times. **(30 sts)**

R6   *Inc, sc 4* 6 times. **(36 sts)**

R7   *Sc 5, inc* 6 times. **(42 sts)**

R8   *Inc, sc 6* 6 times. **(48 sts)**

R9   *Sc 7, inc* 6 times. **(54 sts)**

R10   *Inc, sc 8* 6 times. **(60 sts)**

R11   *Sc 9, inc* 6 times. **(66 sts)**

R12   *Inc, sc 10* 6 times. **(72 sts)**

Fasten off and leave tail for sewing. Add the safety eyes, placing them between rounds 7 and 8, about 3 stitches apart. Sew on the mouth. Add felt cheeks. Make sure to place the eyes along one of the straight edges so when it's folded the eyes are centered. *(photos 1+2)*

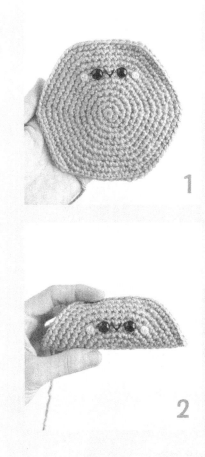

FiLLiNG

Using   Ch 16.

R1   Starting in 2nd ch from hook sc across. **(15 sts)** Ch 1 and turn.

R2-19   Sc 15. Ch 1 and turn. Do not ch 1 and turn after row 19.

This next row will form the wavy sides of the filling.

R2

0   Sc around the entire edge. To do this, begin by placing a sc into the same space as the last sc you just made. *(photo 3)* This will help turn the work so you can work along the sides. Then *hdc dc hdc in one st, sc* 8 times. *(photo 4)* Hdc dc hdc in one st, then inc in the corner space. *(photo 5)* Sc 13, then inc in the corner once more. Then *hdc dc hdc in one st, sc* 9 times. Sc into the fourth corner (this acts as an increase in the corner), then sc 15 across. You should have 105 sts at the end.

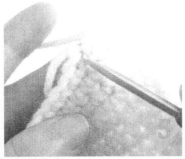

Fasten off and weave in the ends. *(photo 6)*

TO ASSEMBLE THE CANNOLI

1 Roll the filling, starting at the bottom and working your way up. *(photos 7+8)*

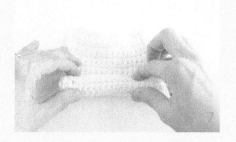

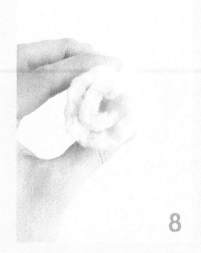

8

2 Place the filling in the center of the cannoli shell. *(photo 9)*

9

3 Fold the shell over the filling, placing the side with the safety eyes on top of the back side. *(photo 10)*

10

4 With the yarn needle, sew the cannoli shell together. Make sure to weave the needle through the stitches of R12 on the shell and not over them. This will create a clean finish. *(photos 11–13)*

5 Secure and hide the tail. *(photos 14+15)*

14

15

CHEESECAKE

MATERIALS

✕ Worsted weight/4-ply yarn:
- Cream
- Golden brown
- Blue
- Red
- Green

✕ Size F/3.75mm crochet hook

✕ 1 pair of 9mm safety eyes for the cheesecake

✕ 2 pairs of 6mm safety eyes for the berries

✕ Black, white, and pink embroidery floss

✕ Small embroidery needle

✕ Fiberfill stuffing

✕ Yarn needle

✕ Stitch marker

✕ Scissors

✕ Thick cardboard *(Optional, but this will make the cheesecake look more realistic, with straight sides)*

ABBREVIATIONS

BLO	Back Loops Only
CH	Chain

INC	Increase
INV DEC	Invisible Decrease
R	Round or Row
SC	Single Crochet
SL ST	Slip Stitch
ST/S	Stitch/es

FINISHED MEASUREMENTS

CHEESECAKE

approx. 4.25 inches wide by 2 inches tall

BLUEBERRY

approx. 1 inch wide by 1 inch tall

STRAWBERRY

approx. 1.5 inches wide by 1.25 inches tall

CHEESECAKE

FiLLiNG

Using *cream yarn*,

R1   6 sc in magic ring. **(6 sts)**

R2   Inc in each st around. **(12 sts)**

R3   *Sc 1, inc* 6 times. **(18 sts)**

R4   *Inc, sc 2* 6 times. **(24 sts)**

R5   *Sc 3, inc* 6 times. **(30 sts)**

R6   *Inc, sc 4* 6 times. **(36 sts)**

R7   *Sc 5, inc* 6 times. **(42 sts)**

R8   *Inc, sc 6* 6 times. **(48 sts)**

R9   *Sc 7, inc* 6 times. **(54 sts)**

R10   *Inc, sc 8* 6 times. **(60 sts)**

R11   In BLO, Sc 60.

R12-17 Sc 60.

Add the 9mm safety eyes, placing them between rounds 14 & 15, about 3 stitches apart. Using black embroidery floss, sew on the mouth.

Change to *golden brown yarn,*

R18   Sc 60.

Fasten off and weave in ends. *(photo 1)*

Trace the top of the cheesecake onto thick cardboard and cut out. Place cardboard inside the cheesecake. *(photos 2+3)* Set aside.

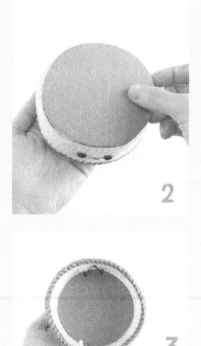

CRUST

Using *golden brown yarn,*

R1   6 sc in magic ring. **(6 sts)**

R2   Inc in each st around. **(12 sts)**

R3   *Sc 1, inc* 6 times. **(18 sts)**

R4   *Inc, sc 2* 6 times. **(24 sts)**

R5   *Sc 3, inc* 6 times. **(30 sts)**

R6   *Inc, sc 4* 6 times. **(36 sts)**

R7   *Sc 5, inc* 6 times. **(42 sts)**

R8   *Inc, sc 6* 6 times. **(48 sts)**

R9   *Sc 7, inc* 6 times. **(54 sts)**

R1
0   *Inc, sc 8* 6 times. **(60 sts)**

Fasten off and leave a long tail for sewing. *(photo 4)* Trace the crust onto thick cardboard and cut it out. You'll want it to be slightly smaller than the crust. It should fit in the center with a little bit of the crust peeking out the sides. *(photo 5)* Set the cardboard piece aside.

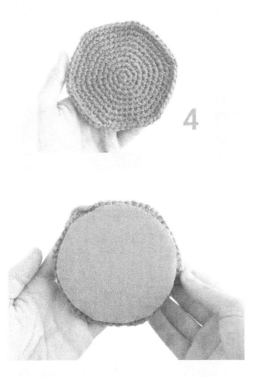

TO ASSEMBLE THE CHEESECAKE

With a yarn needle and tail from crust piece, sew the crust to the bottom of the cheesecake. Weave the needle through the back loops of R18 on the cheesecake and R10 on the crust. *(photos 6+7)* Make sure to weave the needle through the stitches, not over them, to create a clean finish. *(photos*

8+9) Once you're just over halfway around, while there is still enough space to insert the second piece of cardboard, add fiberfill. *(photo 10)* Once you've added enough fiberfill, insert the second piece of cardboard for the bottom of the cheesecake. *(photo 11)* This will contain all the fiberfill in the center and give the top and bottom of the cheesecake a flat surface. Continue sewing the pieces together. Secure and hide the tail. *(photos 12–14)*

8

13

14

BERRIES

BLUEBERRY

MAKE AS MANY AS YOU'D LiKE

Using *blue yarn*,

R1   5 sc in magic ring. **(5 sts)**

R2   Inc in each st around. **(10 sts)**

R3   *Sc 1, inc* 5 times. **(15 sts)**

R4+5   Sc 15.

R6   *Sc 1, inv dec* 5 times. **(10 sts)**

Add the 6mm safety eyes, placing them between rounds 4 and 5, about 2 stitches apart. Using pink embroidery floss, sew on the mouth. Begin adding fiberfill and continue as you close the piece.

R7   Inv dec around 5 times. **(5 sts)**

Fasten off and leave a tail for closing the piece. *(photo 15)*

15

BLUEBERRY TOP

Using *blue yarn,*

R1   5 sc in magic ring. **(5 sts)**

Sl st into first sc to fasten off. Leave a tail for sewing. *(photo 16)*

16

With a yarn needle, sew the top piece to the top of the blueberry. *(photo 17)* Secure and hide the tail.

17

STRAWBERRY

Using *red yarn*,

R1   5 sc in magic ring. **(5 sts)**

R2 Sc 5.

R3 Inc in each st around. **(10 sts)**

R4 Sc 10.

R5 *Sc 1, inc* 5 times. **(15 sts)**

R6 Sc 15.

Add the 6mm safety eyes, placing them between rounds 4 and 5, about 1 stitch apart. Using black embroidery floss, sew on the mouth. Begin adding fiberfill and continue as you close piece.

R7 *Sc 1, inv dec* 5 times. **(10 sts)**

R8 Inv dec around 5 times. **(5 sts)**

Fasten off and leave a tail for closing the piece. *(photo 18)*

18

With white embroidery floss, stitch "seeds" in various places all over the strawberry. *(photo 19)*

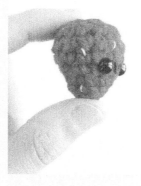

19

LEAFY TOP

Using *green yarn*,

R1   5 sc in magic ring. **(5 sts)**

R2   Inc in each st around. **(10 sts)**

This next round will form the leafy parts. After each leaf is made, make sure to sl st back into the same space as the sc that was made before beginning the chain.

R3   *Sc 2, ch 2 and in 2nd ch from hook sc 1. Sl st back into the same space as the sc that was made before beginning the chain.* 5 times. *(photos 20–23)*

Fasten off and leave a tail for sewing. With a yarn needle, sew the leafy top to the top of the strawberry. *(photo 24)* Make sure to weave the needle between **R2** and **R3** on the top. A horizontal row of stitching will form. *(photo 25)* Secure and hide the tail. *(photo 26)*

Sew the berries to the top of the cheesecake. Secure and hide the tails. *(photos 27+28)*

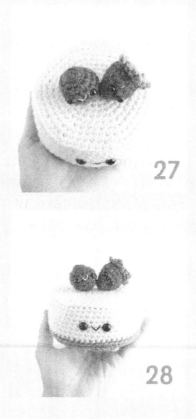

ÉCLAIR

MATERIALS

✖ Worsted weight/4-ply yarn:
  - Tan
  - Brown
  - Cream

✖ Size F/3.75mm crochet hook

✖ 1 pair of 9mm safety eyes

✖ Black embroidery floss

✖ Small embroidery needle

✖ Fiberfill stuffing

✖ Yarn needle

✖ Stitch marker

✖ Scissors

✖ *Optional:* pink felt and thread for cheeks

✖ Straight pins (helpful when assembling the chocolate)

ABBREVIATIONS

CH	Chain
DC	Double Crochet
HDC	Half Double Crochet
INC	Increase

INV DEV	Invisible Decrease
R	Round or Row
SC	Single Crochet
SL ST	Slip Stitch
ST/S	Stitch/es

FINISHED MEASUREMENTS

ÉCLAIR

approx. 5 inches long by 2 inches wide by 2 inches tall

ÉCLAIR

PASTRY

Using *tan yarn*, Ch 19.

In the next row, go through both loops, leaving the back "bump." *(photos 1–3)*

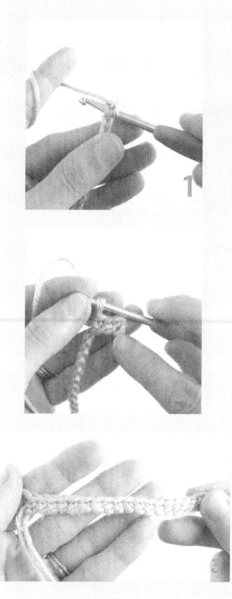

R1 Starting in 2nd ch from hook sc across 18 times, turn, and sc across 18 times in the back "bumps." **(36 sts)** *(photos 4+5)*

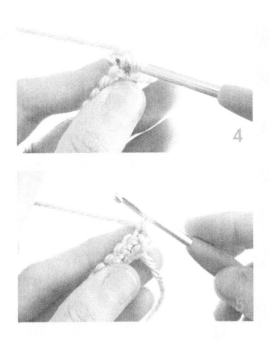

R2 Inc, sc 16, inc in the next 2 sts, sc 16, inc. **(40 sts)** *(photo 6)*

R3 Inc in the next 2 sts, sc 17, inc in the next 3 sts, sc 17, inc. **(46 sts)**

R4 Inc in the next 3 sts, sc 19, inc in the next 4 sts, sc 19, inc. **(54 sts)** *(photo 7)*

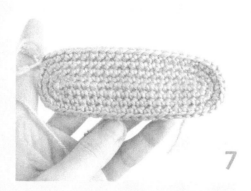

R5-9   Sc 54. *(photo 8)*

R1
0   Sc 54, then sc 1. The extra stitch helps even out the piece. Make sure to move the stitch marker over to the extra added stitch. *(photo 9)*

Add the safety eyes, placing them between rounds 8 and 9, about 3 stitches apart. Sew on the mouth. Add felt cheeks. *(photo 10)*

Inv dec 3 times, sc 19, inv dec 4 times, sc 19, inv dec. **(46 sts)**

Inv dec 2 times, sc 17, inv dec 3 times, sc 17, inv dec. **(40 sts)**
(photos 11+12)

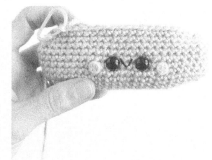

11

12

Fasten off and leave a tail for sewing.

TO ASSEMBLE THE PASTRY

Line up the stitches along the edges. *(photo 13)* With the yarn needle, whipstitch the sides together. *(photos 14+15)* About halfway, add fiberfill to the éclair. *(photo 16)* Continue closing the piece. Secure and hide the tail. *(photos 17+18)*

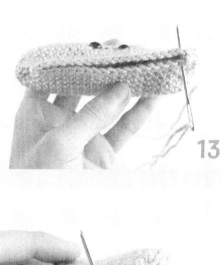

16

17

18

CHOCOLATE

Note: *Refer to photos 1–6 of the pastry pattern—these steps are the same.*

Using **brown yarn,** Ch 19.

In the next row, go through both loops, leaving the back "bump."

R1 Starting in 2nd ch from hook sc across 18 times, turn, and sc across 18 times in the back "bumps." **(36 sts)**

R2 Inc, sc 16, inc in the next 2 sts, sc 16, inc. **(40 sts)**

R3 Inc in the next 2 sts, sc 17, inc in the next 3 sts, sc 17, inc. **(46 sts)**

This next round will form the wavy parts of the chocolate.

R4 *Sc 3, hdc dc, dc hdc, sc 2, hdc dc, dc hdc, sc 3, hdc dc, dc hdc, sc 3, hdc dc, dc hdc, sc 2, hdc dc, dc hdc.* 2 times. **(66 sts)** *(photo 19)*

19

Fasten off and leave a long tail for sewing.

TO SEW THE CHOCOLATE TO THE PASTRY

Pin the chocolate in place with straight pins. *(photos 20+21)* With a yarn needle, sew the chocolate to the pastry. Make sure to weave the needle through the stitches of R4 on the chocolate and not over them. *(photos 22+23)* This will create a clean edge along the chocolate. Secure and hide the tail. *(photos 24+25)*

20

24

25

CREAM

MAKE 2

Using *cream yarn*,

R1 6 sc in magic ring. **(6 sts)**

Sl st into the first sc to fasten off. Leave a tail for sewing. *(photo 26)*

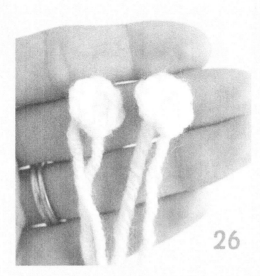

26

With a yarn needle, sew the cream pieces to the sides of the pastry. Secure and hide the tails. *(photos 27+28)*

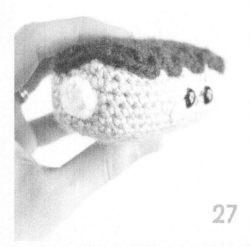

27

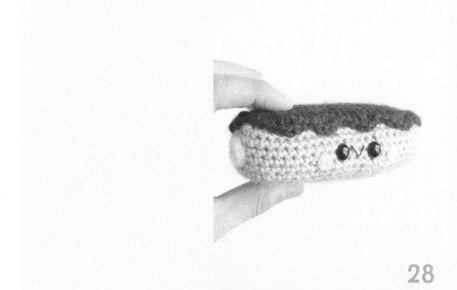

28

MATERIALS

✗ Worsted weight/4-ply yarn:
- Pink or mint green
- Tan
- Red
- Green
- Brown

✗ Size G/4mm crochet hook

✗ 2 pairs of 6mm safety eyes

✗ Black embroidery floss

✗ Small embroidery needle

✗ Fiberfill stuffing

✗ Yarn needle

✗ Stitch marker

✗ Scissors

ABBREVIATIONS

CH	Chain
DC	Double Crochet
FLO	Front Loops Only
HDC	Half Double Crochet
INC	Increase

INV DEC	Invisible Decrease
R	Round or Row
SC	Single Crochet
SL ST	Slip Stitch
ST/S	Stitch/es
TR	Treble Crochet

FINISHED MEASUREMENTS

ICE CREAM CONE

approx. 3 inches wide by 4.5 inches tall

CONE

Using *tan yarn,*

R1   6 sc in magic ring. **(6 sts)**

R2   *Sc 1, inc* 3 times. **(9 sts)**

R3   Sc 9.

R4   *Sc 2, inc* 3 times. **(12 sts)**

R5   Sc 12.

R6   *Sc 3, inc* 3 times. **(15 sts)**

R7   Sc 15.

R8   *Sc 4, inc* 3 times. **(18 sts)**

R9   Sc 18.

R10   *Sc 5, inc* 3 times. **(21 sts)**

R11   Sc 21.

R12   *Sc 6, inc* 3 times. **(24 sts)**

R13   Sc 24.

Add the safety eyes, placing them between rounds 11 and 12, about 3 stitches apart. Sew on the mouth.

R1
4   *Sc 7, inc* 3 times. **(27 sts)**

R1
5   Sc 27.

R1
6   *Sc 8, inc* 3 times. **(30 sts)**

R1
7   Sc 30.

Fasten off and leave a long tail for sewing. *(photo 1)*

1

iCE CREAM

Using **pink** or *mint green yarn,*

R1   6 sc in magic ring. **(6 sts)**

R2   Inc in each st around. **(12 sts)**

R3   *Sc 1, inc* 6 times. **(18 sts)**

R4   *Sc 2, inc* 6 times. **(24 sts)**

R5   *Sc 3, inc* 6 times. **(30 sts)**

R6   *Sc 4, inc* 6 times. **(36 sts)**

R7-10   Sc 36.

Sc 4, inv dec 6 times. **(30 sts)**

In FLO, *3 hdc in one st, sc in the next st* 15 times. **(60 sts)** *(photos 2+3)*

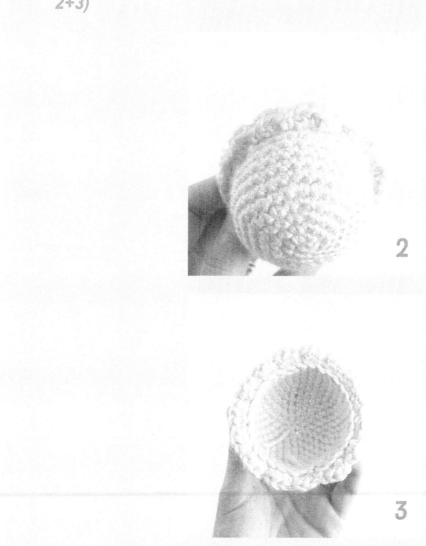

Fasten off and weave in the end. *(photo 4)*

4

With red or brown yarn, sew "strawberry" or "chocolate" pieces in various places all over the ice cream. *(photo 5)*

5

TO ASSEMBLE THE ICE CREAM CONE

Add fiberfill to the cone first. *(photo 6)* Then weave the yarn needle through the last row of stitches in R17 of the cone and the back loops leftover in R12 of the ice cream. Make sure to weave the needle through the stitches on the cone and not over them. *(photos 7–9)* A horizontal row of stitches will form at the very top to make a clean finish. *(photo 10)* Before closing the piece, add more fiberfill to the ice cream cone. Secure and hide the tail. *(photo 11)*

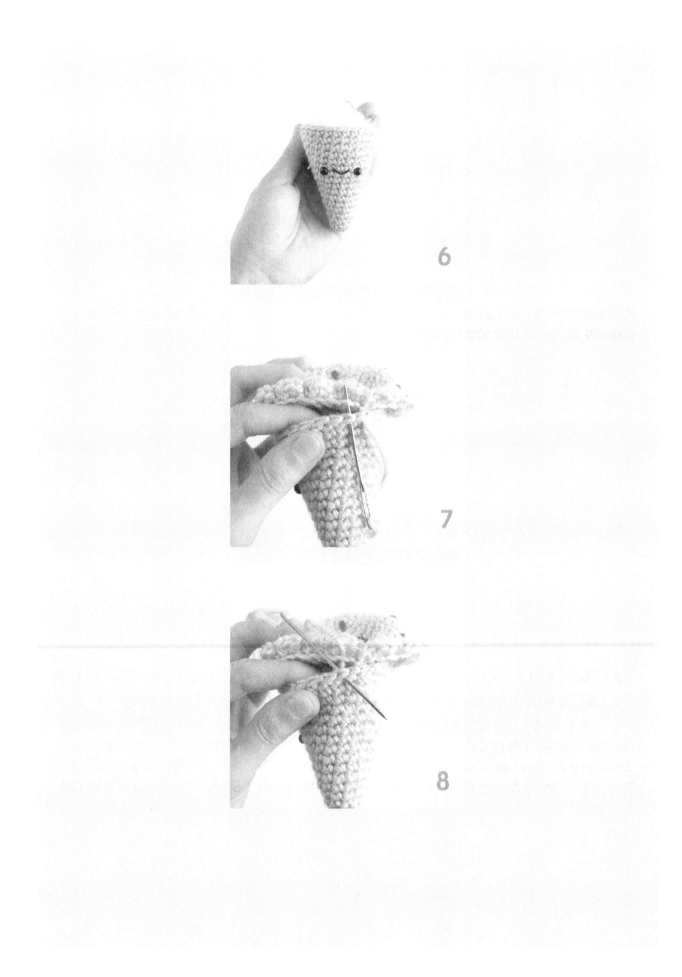

6

7

8

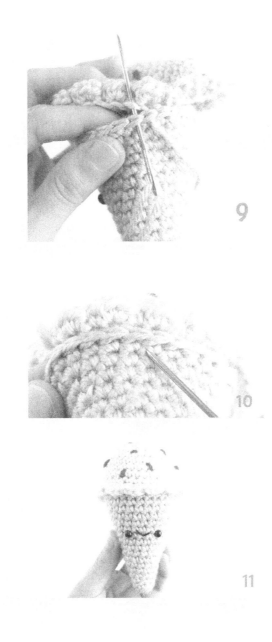

9

10

11

CHOCOLATE SAUCE

Using *brown yarn,*

R1   6 sc in magic ring. **(6 sts)**

R2   Inc in each st around. **(12 sts)**

R3   *Sc 1, inc* 6 times. **(18 sts)**

R4   *Sc 2, inc* 6 times. **(24 sts)**

R5   *Sc 3, inc* 6 times. **(30 sts)**

R6   *Sc 4, inc* 6 times. **(36 sts)**

This next round will form the ripples around the edge.

R7   Sc 3, hdc dc, dc hdc, sc 4, hdc dc, 2 dc, dc hdc, sc 4, hdc dc, 2 tr, dc hdc, sc 4, hdc dc, dc hdc, sc 4, hdc dc, 2 dc, dc hdc, sc 4. **(49 sts)**

Fasten off and leave a long tail for sewing. *(photo 12)* With a yarn needle, sew the chocolate to the top of the ice cream. *(photo 13)* Weave the needle through the stitches of R7 and not over them. *(photo 14)* This will create a clean finish on the chocolate. Secure and hide the tail. *(photo 15)*

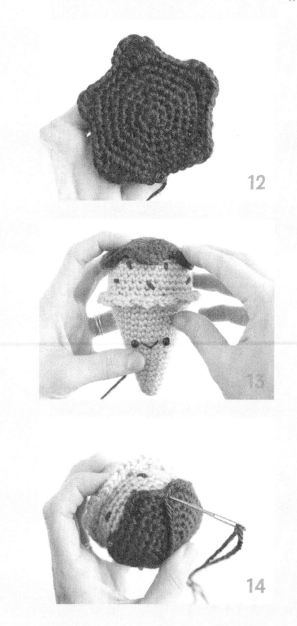

15

CHERRY

Using *red yarn*,

R1   5 sc in magic ring. **(5 sts)**

R2   Inc in each st around. **(10 sts)**

R3   *Sc 1, inc* 5 times. **(15 sts)**

R4+5   Sc 15.

R6   *Sc 1, inv dec* 5 times. **(10 sts)**

Add the safety eyes, placing them between rounds 4 and 5, about 2 stitches apart. Sew on the mouth. Begin adding fiberfill and continue as you close the piece.

R7   Inv dec around 5 times. **(5 sts)**

Fasten off and leave a tail for closing the piece. Save the tail for sewing the cherry to the chocolate. *(photo 16)*

16

CHERRY STEM

Using *green yarn,* Ch 7.

R1 Starting in 2nd ch from hook sl st across. **(6 sts)**

Fasten off and leave a tail for sewing. *(photo 17)*

17

With a yarn needle, sew the stem to the top of the cherry. Secure and hide the tail. *(photo 18)* Sew the cherry on top of the chocolate sauce. Secure and hide the tail. *(photo 19)*

18

19

PIE

MATERIALS

X Worsted weight/4-ply yarn:
  - Tan
  - Blue or red
  - Gray

X Size F/3.75 mm crochet hook

X 1 pair of 9mm safety eyes

X Black embroidery floss

X Small embroidery needle

X Fiberfill stuffing

X Yarn needle

X Stitch marker

X Scissors

X *Optional:* pink felt and thread for cheeks

X Straight pins (helpful when assembling pieces)

X Thick cardboard (Optional, but this will make the pie tin flatter)

ABBREVIATIONS

BLO	Back Loops Only
Ch	Chain
DC	Double Crochet

FLO	Front Loops Only
HDC	Half Double Crochet
INC	Increase
R	Round or Row
SC	Single Crochet
ST/S	Stitch/es

FINISHED MEASUREMENTS

PIE

approx. 5 inches wide by 3 inches tall

PIE TIN

Using *gray yarn,*

R1   6 sc in magic ring. **(6 sts)**

R2   Inc in each st around. **(12 sts)**

R3   *Sc 1, inc* 6 times. **(18 sts)**

R4   *Inc, sc 2* 6 times. **(24 sts)**

R5   *Sc 3, inc* 6 times. **(30 sts)**

R6   *Inc, sc 4* 6 times. **(36 sts)**

R7   *Sc 5, inc* 6 times. **(42 sts)**

R8   *Inc, sc 6* 6 times. **(48 sts)**

R9   *Sc 7, inc* 6 times. **(54 sts)**

R10   *Inc, sc 8* 6 times. **(60 sts)**

R11   *Sc 9, inc* 6 times. **(66 sts)**

R12   In BLO, *Sc 10, inc* 6 times. **(72 sts)**

R13-18   Sc 72.

Fasten off and weave in the ends. Add the safety eyes, placing them between rounds 15 and 16, about 4 stitches apart. Sew on the mouth. Add felt cheeks. *(photo 1)*

Trace the bottom of the pie tin on thick cardboard and cut it out. *(photo 2)* Place the cardboard inside the tin. *(photo 3)* Set aside.

FILLING

Using *blue* or *red yarn*,

R1   6 sc in magic ring. **(6 sts)**

R2   Inc in each st around. **(12 sts)**

R3   *Sc 1, inc* 6 times. **(18 sts)**

R4   *Inc, sc 2* 6 times. **(24 sts)**

R5   *Sc 3, inc* 6 times. **(30 sts)**

R6   *Inc, sc 4* 6 times. **(36 sts)**

R7   *Sc 5, inc* 6 times. **(42 sts)**

R8   *Inc, sc 6* 6 times. **(48 sts)**

R9   *Sc 7, inc* 6 times. **(54 sts)**

R10   *Inc, sc 8* 6 times. **(60 sts)**

R11   *Sc 9, inc* 6 times. **(66 sts)**

R12   *Inc, sc 10* 6 times. **(72 sts)**

Change to *tan yarn,*

R13   Sc 72. *(photo 4)*

4

R1

4   In FLO, *Sc 1, hdc dc hdc in one st, sc 1* 24 times. **(120 sts)** *(photos 5+6)*

5

6

Fasten off and leave an extra-long tail for sewing.

TO ASSEMBLE THE PiE

With a yarn needle and the tail from the filling piece, sew the filling to the pie tin. Weave the needle through the back loops of R18 on the pie tin and the back loops leftover from R14 on the filling. *(photos 7–9)*, Make sure to add fiberfill before completely closing the piece. *(photo 10)* When adding fiberfill, add enough that the top forms a slight dome. *(photo 11)* Secure and hide the tail. *(photo 12)*

9

10

11

12

LATTICE WORK

MAKE 10 STRIPS TOTAL

(photos 13+14)

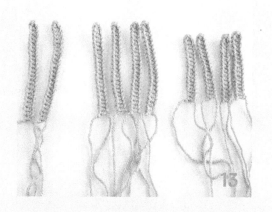

URGE STRIP

MAKE 2

Using *tan yarn*, Ch 25.

R1   Starting in 2nd ch from hook hdc across. **(24 sts)**

Fasten off and leave a long tail for sewing.

MEDIUM STRIP

MAKE 4

Using *tan yarn,* Ch 23.

R1   Starting in 2nd ch from hook hdc across. **(22 sts)**

Fasten off and leave a long tail for sewing.

SMALL STRIP

MAKE 4

Using *tan yarn,* Ch 17.

R1   Starting in 2nd ch from hook hdc across. **(16 sts)**

Fasten off and leave a long tail for sewing.

TO ASSEMBLE THE LATTICE WORK

Reference the photos while assembling! The strips go over and under each other, and the photos illustrate which ones go where. Make sure to only sew the ends of the strips.

1. Place both large strips in the middle of the pie, in a "plus sign" (+). *(photo 15)* It's best to keep the safety eyes facing forward while placing the strips.

15

2 Take two of the medium strips and place them on the sides of the vertical large strip. Place them under the horizontal large strip. *(photo 16)*

16

3 Take the remaining two medium strips and place them on the sides of the horizontal large strip. Place them under the two vertical medium strips and over the vertical large strip. *(photo 17)*

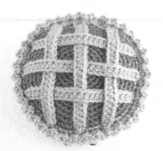

17

4 Next, take two of the small strips and place them on the sides of the horizontal medium strips. They will go over the two vertical medium strips and under the vertical large strip. *(photo 18)*

18

5 Take the remaining two small strips and place on the sides of the vertical medium strips. They will go under the two horizontal medium strips and over the horizontal large strip. *(photo 19)*

19

6 After sewing each end, secure and hide the tails. *(photos 20–22)*

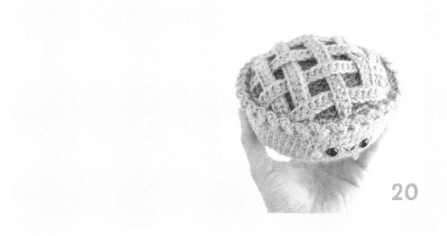

20

21

22

Made in the USA
Las Vegas, NV
18 October 2024

97053142R00299